A Word to the Aged

by

William Bridge

Edited by Dr. Don Kistler

Soli Deo Gloria Publications
... *for instruction in righteousness* ...

Soli Deo Gloria Publications
A division of Soli Deo Gloria Ministries, Inc.
P. O. Box 451, Morgan PA 15064
(412) 221-1901/FAX 221-1902
www.SDGbooks.com

*

A Word to the Aged was published in 1679. This reprint, in which spelling, grammar, and formatting changes have been made, is ©2003 by Soli Deo Gloria. All rights reserved. Printed in the USA.

*

ISBN 1-57358-154-2

*

Library of Congress Cataloging-in-Publication Data

Bridge, William, 1600?-1670.
A word to the aged / by William Bridge ; edited by Don Kistler.
p. cm.
Originally published: 1679.
ISBN 1-57358-154-2 (pbk. : alk. paper)
1. Aged–Conduct of life. 2. Christian aged–Religious life. 3. Aging–Religious aspects–Christianity. I. Kistler, Don. II. Title
BJ1691 .B7 2003
248.8'5–dc22
2003017543

A Word to the Aged

The Old Man's Weakness
There is no state or condition of men but some grace, goodness or virtue may and can plant upon, just as there is no condition but some sin will grow upon.

Yet there is some grace or virtue that is most suited unto some condition and will grow best upon such a soil. Therefore the Apostle John says, "I write unto you, fathers, because ye have known Him that is from the beginning. I write unto you, young men, because ye have overcome the wicked one. I write unto you, little children, because ye have known the Father" (1 John 2:13). It is our wisdom, therefore, to observe what our state and soil is and to plant our ground accordingly. Now old age is a dry and barren ground. The state of old age is a state of weakness and of much infirmity. Solomon calls it "the evil day" in Ecclesiastes 12.

Old age is evil in regard of natural and moral infirmities. It is evil in regard of natural infirmities, for then "the clouds return after the rain." In the time of youth, if a man is sick, and that cloud has emptied itself by some great sickness, he is well again, and a fair day of health is upon him. But if a man is stricken with years, and a cloud of sickness arises upon him, though that cloud has discharged itself by some great distemper, yet still it rains in upon him, and he can hardly sit dry in his old cottage. Therefore Solomon says of this evil day that then "the clouds return after the rain." Then, also, the sun and moon and stars are darkened (verse 2), that is, the reason, memory, fancy, and all those faculties which receive and give out our reason. "When the keepers of the house shall tremble," that is, the hands and the arms; "and the strong men shall bow themselves," that is, the thighs and legs; "and the grinders cease because they are few," that is, the teeth; "and those that look out of the windows be darkened," that is, the eyes (verse 3). "The doors shall be shut in the streets when the sound of the grinding is low," that is, the lips are shut and kept closed lest the meat should fall out of the mouth through want of teeth; "and all the daughters of music shall be brought low," that is, both the speech and hearing" (verse 4). Then "the almond tree shall flourish," that is, the head grows gray and hoary; "a grasshopper shall be a burden," for an old man cannot bear the lightest burden; "desire fails," that is, the appetite for meat, drink, and the marriage bed (verse 5). Then "the silver cord is loosed," that is, the marrow of the back; and "the golden bowl is broken," that is, the skull, which is round, yellow, and contains and preserves the brain; and "the pitcher is broken at the fountain," that is, the bladder which held the urine, which in old age insensibly passes away; and "the wheel is broken at the cistern," that is, the lungs are broken off from their motion of respiration or inspiration by phlegm from the stomach, or the circulation of the blood is interrupted or hindered (verse 6). Thus the natural infirmities of an old man are very many, and the day of old age is an evil day in that respect. Yea, upon this account, an old man is but half a man, "for eyes hath he, and seeth not; ears hath he, and heareth not."

But as the day of old age is an evil day in regard of

A Word to the Aged

natural infirmities, so it is in regard of moral ones:

Then men are apt to be too drowsy and remiss in the things of God.

Then they are apt to be too covetous and tenacious for the things of the world. As wantonness is the young man's vice, so covetousness is the old man's sin.

Then they are apt to be too timorous and fearful. We read but of one man who came to Christ by night out of fear, and he was a rich and old man, Nicodemus.

Then are they apt to be too touchy, peevish, angry and forward; for old age is a continued sickness, and in sickness men are apt to be angry.

Then are they also unapt to be taught, and are very unteachable; they think that they know more than others, and that they are not now to learn (Ecclesiastes 4:13).

Then they are hard to please.

Then they are full of complaints of the present times, praising the days of old. And the old men of those days complained as much in their day as these do of the present one.

And of all men, they are the most impenitent, for by custom and long continuance in sin they are the most hardened, and so are the least penitent.

They are apt also to think and speak of the sins of their youth with delight, and so to commit those things again by thought and word which they cannot commit by action.

They are full of suspicions and very apt to surmise, suspect, and fear the worst, for experience, giving notice of former dangers, keeps their souls in continual alarm.

Having and laboring under all these and other infirmities, both natural and moral, a threefold work is incumbent upon the aged: first, to comfort and bear up themselves against their natural infirmities; second, to strengthen themselves against their moral infirmities and to root them out; and third, to plant that positive grace and goodness in the room thereof which best suits their soil and condition.

The Old Man's Staff
Comforts against the natural infirmities of old age are many. Christ Himself bore them, and still, as our High Priest, sympathizes with us under them. He singled out those aged infirmities for His care and cure when He was here on earth (John 5). There were many who laid by the pool of Bethesda; among them was one that had lain sick and diseased for thirty-eight years; a young man, therefore, he was not. He would have stepped into the pool, but others stepped in before him, and he had no man to help him. He was a poor neglected man, whom others did not mind. Yet this was the man whom Christ came to cure, whom Christ minded, sought out, and cured. Though you may be a poor neglected old person, and have lain long under your infirmities, yet Christ has a cure for you. The blind men cried, and their cries led Christ to show mercy (Mathew 20:31–32).

Though your infirmities are never too many and great, yet you have a peculiar honor that is twisted with your infirmity, for it is called "the crown of old age." In times of the Old Testament, they were to rise up and bow before the ancient; yea, it is our duty to honor them, for this honor is joined and commanded with the fear of God. Leviticus 19:32: "Thou shalt rise up before the hoary head, and honor the face of the old man, and fear thy God; I am the Lord." The fear of God and honoring the old man is commanded with the same breath, and linked together in the same sentence.

Though you are very aged, yet you may be very good. Was not Eli very good, yet very aged? Was not David very good, yet he was very old when he said, "Lord, now lettest Thou thy servant depart in peace"? Was not Anna very good, yet she was very aged? Who does not know what a good man Paul was, yet he called himself "Paul the aged"? Good John was aged John. Possibly, then, you may be very good, though you are very aged, laboring under much infirmity.

And though your flesh is weak, yet your spirit may be willing. "The flesh indeed is weak," said Christ, when His disciples slept through natural infirmity. It was late at night and they were full of grief. "But the spirit is willing," said He also; and where the spirit is willing, He will pass by the weakness of the flesh and accept the willingness of the spirit.

These infirmities of old age are such as are not the fruit of our own sin. The more any infirmity is caused by sin, the more afflictive it is, for sin is the sting of death. I confess, indeed, they may be sometimes, for the sins of youth sometimes bite sore in age. "I ate so much of the forbidden fruit," said a good man, "when I was young that God was fain to give me wormseed to kill the worm." But the infirmities of old age are generally the decays of nature, not of grace.

They are good warnings of our change approaching, and by them we die daily, that at last we may die graciously and comfortably.

And who are those to whom God reveals Himself but His old friends; those He will acquaint with His secrets, and make known His mind unto? Job 12:12: "With the ancient is wisdom; and in length of days understanding."

Though your legs are weak, yet they may be strong enough to carry you to heaven, that better country, which you are now going to, and are very near; indeed your own present country is a good country, but the country you are now going to is a better country (Hebrews 11:16). It is:

• Better in regard of buildings: "Whose builder and maker is God" (Hebrews 11:10).

• Better in regard of inhabitants: "Where no unclean thing doth enter" (Revelation 21:27).

• Better in regard of quietness and freedom from trouble: where all tears shall not only be wiped from our cheeks, but out of our eyes, as the Greek word bears it in Revelation 7:17, insomuch as the eye shall never breed a tear again, nor be the womb of tears.

• Better in regard of riches: where you shall have "an inheritance incorruptible, undefiled, that fadeth not away."

• Better in regard of pleasure: for, says the psalmist, "At Thy right hand are rivers of pleasures, and that forevermore."

• Better in regard of largeness: for if the whole earth is but a pin's head in comparison to the heavens, then surely there is room enough in heaven for every one to enjoy a greater kingdom than all England amounts unto.

• Better in regard of self-subsistence: here one country depends upon another, but heaven is that country alone which depends upon no other country.

• Better in regard of our freedom from needs and necessities. It was Augustine's prayer, "Deliver me, O Lord, from my necessities." It is a great mercy now to have bread to eat when we want it, but it is a greater mercy to have no need of it. It is a great mercy to have a good bed to lie on, and so to sleep quietly, but it is a greater mercy to have no need of bed or sleep. This is the state of that heavenly country, where you do not have these blessings, but you have no need of them.

• Better also is it in regard of continuance, where every mercy and blessing grows upon the stalk of eternity. And if it is a good thing to have a lease of a good house and land for a hundred years, what a blessed thing then it is to have a glorious mansion and inheritance lying in the fields of eternity? When you come to a great palace and see fair barns and stables and outhouses, you say then, "If the outrooms and stables are so costly and sumptuous, how costly and glorious is this palace within?" Yet this is that country, that better country that you are going and drawing nigh unto, and your passage to that place is very short; for no sooner do you step out of this world but, if you are godly, gracious, and in Christ, you step immediately into that country. There is no sleeping of the soul after death. Some have dreamed of such a sleep, but Solomon tells us that the body upon death goes to the dust, and the spirit unto Him who gave it (Ecclesiastes 12:7). Christ said to the thief, "This day shalt thou be with Me in paradise." And the Apostle Paul tells us that paradise and the third heaven are one and the same thing (2 Corinthians 12). Yea, says Paul, "I am in a strait betwixt two, not having a desire to depart for mine own enjoyment, or to live for the service of the churches" (Philippians 1:23–24). Whereas, if the soul slept in the grave with the body, he needed not to have been in that strait. "I desire," said he, "to be dissolved, and to be with Christ." If with Christ presently, how can the soul sleep with the body in the dust? "For we know," he says, "that if our earthly house of this tabernacle were dissolved, we have a building of God, an house not made with hands, eternal in the heavens" (2 Corinthians 5:1). Though your turf house now is ready to fire into a fever with every spark of distemper, is there not enough in that house above to pay for all? Surely there is. Why, then, should you not lift up your heads, you old men, and be of good comfort under all your natural infirmities?

And as for your moral infirmities, if you would strengthen yourself against them and root out these weeds there, be sure that you study and think much on Christ crucified, who alone is our righteousness and our strength. Temptations or sins blown out by reason or resolution will easily light again; but quench them in the blood of Christ, and they light no more. When the Israelite was stung with fiery serpents, he did not stand looking at his swollen arm or leg, but on the brazen serpent, and so was cured. Christ lifted upon the cross is our brazen serpent, and He has said, "Look unto Me, oh, all ye ends of the earth, and be saved."

Then by way of consideration, think, and think much with yourselves, what an evil thing it is to sin when a man is ready to die. Thus you do not leave your sin, but your sin (leaves) you.

Be sure that you do not chew the cud of your former sins by musing on them with delight, for thereby you justify your former practice; but rather mourn over them, for the way to keep from future sins is to mourn for former ones. And the way to be kept from sins of old age is to mourn for the sins of our youth.

But, above all things, under your study of Christ crucified, be sure that you strengthen your love for God in Christ; for if the boughs of the tree are weak, the way to strengthen them is not to carry up dung to the boughs but to lay the dung to the root; for by strengthening the root, you strengthen the branches. Now the root of all our mortification is love, for love is the cause of hatred. "Ye that love the Lord, hate evil." Love for God eats out our love to sin, as the fear of God eats out our fear of men; and your love for God is strengthened by the sight of His love for you. For love is the cause of love; the more we see God's love for us, the more we love Him, and the more we hate our sins. Would you, therefore, take up your sinful weeds by the roots? Then strengthen your love, and this shall be a staff in your hand to strengthen and bear you up under all your infirmities, both natural and moral.

The Old Man's Guide

But there is yet one thing remaining and incumbent on the aged, and that is to plant the positive grace and virtue which best suits his soil and condition.

What are those good things, therefore, that old men especially are to do in their old age?

They are full of experience, and therefore, should be full of faith; for though God's Word only is the ground of our faith, yet experience is a great help to faith. Now there is a faith of reliance and a faith of assurance. Faith of reliance justifies; faith of assurance comforts. Old men, therefore, are to exercise the faith of reliance, relying upon Christ's righteousness, renouncing their own. And they are to exercise the faith of assurance, for it is ill dying with a doubting soul. As zeal is the young man's virtue, so faith is the old man's grace.

It is their work and duty to renew their repentance, for they are shortly to appear before the Lord, and to give an account of all that they have done in the flesh. And will they appear before him in their filthy rags? Now, though we are only washed from our sins by the blood of Christ unto justification, yet we are washed from our filth by the hand of repentance unto sanctification. For as God promises to wash us with clean water, so He commands us to wash ourselves in Isaiah 1. And if a man will not wash and repent at the last, when will he repent? When the leaves are off the trees, we see the birds' nests in the trees and bushes. Now in our old age our leaves are off; then therefore we may see those nests of sin and lust in our hearts and lives which we did not see before, and so be sensible and repent of them.

They are also to be much in reading the Scripture, in meditation, and in prayer. By reading they shall gain knowledge; by meditation on their reading they shall add affection to their knowledge; and by prayer they shall add devotion to their affection.

Because the elderly are ready to weigh anchor and set sail for the other world, it will be good for them to observe what the proper work of this world is, and to be much therein. For "every thing is beautiful in the time thereof." Now is a time for believing. Heaven is no time for faith, for in heaven we live by sight. Now is a time for repentance; in heaven there is no repentance for there is no sorrow. Now is a time of patience; in heaven there is no patience under affliction for there is no affliction. Now is a time of hearing the Word preached, and for sacraments and ordinances; there is no preaching, sacraments, or ordinances in heaven. Now is a time to relieve the poor; in heaven there is no room for such charity; it is that country where no beggar lies at your door. Now is a time to observe our relations; in heaven there are no such relations, for "they neither marry nor are given in marriage, but are as the angels." Now, therefore, whatever is in the power of your hand to do, do it with all your might; for in the grave there is no work, nor in heaven there is none of this work. Therefore, what is to be done here, and cannot be done there, is now to be done especially.

It is the old man's duty to live much in a little time, and to be more exact and strict in his life than ever; for the nearer the stone comes to the center, the faster it moves. The more wisdom any man has, the more exactly he works. Wisdom and exactness go together: "See that you walk exactly, not as fools, but as wise," says the apostle. Now gray hairs should be found in the way of wisdom; and the more frequently a man works, the more exactly he may do the same. Now those who are ancient have (or should have) been frequently in holy duties; they therefore, of all men, are to live and walk most exactly. Thus it shall not be said of them, as Seneca says of one, "He did not live long, but he was long."

Then they are to knock off from the world, and to use the world as if they used it not. "For the fashion of this world passeth away, and the time is short, therefore their moderation should be known unto all men, for the Lord is at hand." If a tooth is to be taken, and the gum is cut, the tooth comes out with ease; but if it is fast set in the gum, and not first loosened from the gum, it comes out with much difficulty. And what is the reason that many die with such difficulty? Because they are so fast set in their worldly gums; they are not loosened from their relations. Therefore, it is good for old men, who are upon the brink of death, to loosen themselves from this world and all their relations.

Let the old man take heed of all these evils that may and will stain the glory of his old age. All sins leave a blot and stain behind them; but youthful sins especially stain old age, for the sin is the greater, as it is more contrary to the sinner. It is an evil thing for any man to be unjust, but worse for a judge to be so, because there is a special repugnancy between the sin and the sinner. There is a special repugnancy between old men and youthful sins. Give me a young man indeed with an old man's virtue, wisdom. Give me an old man indeed with a young man's grace, zeal. But a young man vitiated with an old man's sin, covetousness, and an old man defiled with a young man's sin, wantonness, are each an abomination to both God and man, and are stained deeply and greatly. A certain Lacedaemonian was asked why he allowed his beard to grow so long. He replied, "To the end that, looking on my white hairs, I may be put in mind not to do any act unbeseeming my hoary whiteness."

It is their duty also to prepare for death, their great change and dissolution. It was the complaint of Caesar Borgius: "When I lived, I provided for everything but death; now I am ready to die, I am not provided to die." Shall I provide for other journeys, and not for this great journey? This is every man's work, but the old man's especially. For though the young man's candle may go out, the old man's will and shall.

But what should the old man do so that he may be

fit to die?

God will give dying grace upon dying ground. Yet, that aged person must be sure to do the work of his present day. The only way to be fit for the work of the morrow is to do the work of the present day.

Let him examine himself and make his reckonings even with God so that, when he comes to die, he may have nothing to do but to die.

Let him resign and give himself and his will to God afresh. Thus Christ did as soon as He drew nigh to death. "If it be possible," said He, "let this cup pass; yet not My will, but Thy will be done." This He did again and again, at His first approach unto death; and this He did in His last words: "Father, into Thy hands I commend My spirit."

Let him long after heaven and not be afraid to die; for if he is in Christ, death itself is his. "All things are yours," said the apostle, "life and death, for ye are Christ's." And who is afraid of what is his own? The child is not afraid of the great mastiff, but puts his hands into the dog's mouth; and if you ask him why, he will tell you, "For he is our own dog." Now if a man is in Christ, this great mastiff, death, is his own, and therefore why should he be afraid? Yea, why should he not be willing to die? Was Elijah unwilling to go into the fiery chariot? Is the child unwilling to ride home because it is a trotting horse that he must ride upon? No. Though it is a hard and a sore sickness that you must ride on, yet, if it carries you home to your Father, why should you be unwilling to die?

Now, the only way to be willing to die is to get assurance of your interest in Christ and of your own salvation. What is the reason that men are unwilling to die but because they cannot tell where they shall land after death. "True," says one, "I am launching forth into the ocean of eternity; but on what shore I shall land, only God knows. Oh, that I might live one year more, one month more, yea, one hour more, until I had assurance of my salvation." And when that comes, then the soul, having thereby gotten Christ into his arms, cries out and says, "Lord, now lettest Thy servant depart in peace, for mine eyes have seen Thy salvation."

Let him also set his house in order, make his will, and leave his legacies to his children, friends and posterity. Shall Achitopel, when he changed himself, set his house in order before he died; and shall not an elderly Christian set his house and heart in order, make his will, and leave his legacies unto his friends and posterity?

The Old Man's Will and Legacies

But what good thing should the old leave or give unto his posterity by his last will?

Why, first, he must be sure to give his soul unto God while he lives; for if a man gives his soul to the world and devil while he lives, what right has he to give it unto God when he dies? If I give away a house or land while I live, can I justly give it to another when I die? And if I give away my soul to sin, world, or devil while I live, how can I justly give it to God when I die?

Let him leave a good example unto his posterity; a good example is a great legacy. Thus a man speaks when he is dead, as Abel does (Hebrews 11:4).

If he would leave some good things unto his posterity, let him leave his experiences. An old man is, or

A Word to the Aged

should be, rich in experience; an ancient Christian is, or should be, an experimental Christian. When therefore he comes to die, it is his work and duty to leave those experiences to his posterity.

Yea, let him leave some good exhortations and admonitions with and upon his posterity, saying, "Come, O my son, my daughter, my friend, I am now going the way of all flesh; when I am gone, be sure that you fear the Lord and keep His commandments, for if you keep God's commandments, you shall have the comfort of His promises. Be sure, also, my son, that you give your first and best unto God; for God is the first and best of beings, and if you honor the Lord with your substance, and with the first-fruits of all your increase; then shall your barns be filled with plenty, and your presses shall burst forth with new wine (Proverbs 3:10). And why would you not give your first time and best of your all unto God, who has given His best and only Son unto you? If you serve God while you are young, God will bless you when you are old; and if you come unto Him when you are young, He will not forsake you when you are old.

Thus David argued, "O God, forsake me not, now I am old and gray headed" (Psalms 71:18). Why? Verse 17: "Thou hast taught me from my youth." Verse 5: "For Thou art my hope, O Lord God. Thou art my trust from my youth." God is engaged, it seems, by this argumentation (to those who are good while they are young) to show mercy to them when they are old. The hand of a child may pull up a plant when it is young and tender, but if it grows to be a tall tree, all the horses in the town cannot pluck it up.

You can hear David exhorting his children: "So in

regard of sin, let your mortification of sin therefore begin early. If the paper is clear and clean, you may write anything on it; but if other things are scribbled on the paper, it is then unfit to receive any writing or impression. So it is in regard of the impression of good upon the soul and heart. Let your vivification, therefore, and holiness, begin early. Thus let your first be given unto God.

"And though you have not so great parts and gifts as others have, yet let your desires of good be as full as any others. What you want in expression make up in affection. When nature is wanting in one thing, it supplies it in another. The blind man has the best memory. And that God who gives you a heart to desire will give you your heart's desire. If your parts are taller by head and shoulders than others, then expect envy, and pray much for humility.

"In case you sin at any time, as you will often, then be sure, O my children, that you delay not your repentance, for the green wound is most easily cured. The thief indeed was converted at the last, but it was as soon as he was called. Some come in at the last hour of the day, but they come when they are called. Now you are called today, and therefore defer it not until tomorrow.

Let your company be good, for every man is as the company of his choice is. Ecclesiastes 12:1: 'Remember now thy Creator in the days of thy youth,' which, if you please, you may read according to the Hebrew, 'In the days of the choice, or choices,' because in the days of youth a man makes choice of a trade or calling. Then he makes choice of his religion, then he makes choice of his wife, and then makes choice of his company. Now then, my son, have a care of these choices.

"And let your discourse be always seasoned with salt, for, 'By your words you shall be justified, and by your words you shall be condemned at the last day,' says our Savior; for words are the index of the mind. A good soul never lives at the sign of ill speech.

"And as for the world and the things thereof, though you may pray for much, yet you must be content with little. The way to have a mercy or blessing is to be content to go without it; and the way to avoid any evil is to submit to it; and to remove it is to bless God over it, as Job did.

"Let your recreation, O my children, be sparing, for they are but your sauce, and not your nourishment, your cordial, or your steady diet.

"Of all books, study the Bible; of all duties, be much in prayer; of all graces, exercise faith; of all days, observe the Lord's day; and of all things in heaven and earth, be sure that you get an interest in God by Jesus Christ.

"And by any means, O my children, and friends, 'let brotherly love continue, for love is the fulfilling of the law.' Who can break a faggot when sticks are joined together by the common band? But if the sticks are parted, how easily they are all broken. And what is the reason that such judicial breaches are made upon us, but because our pride and want of love makes such sinful breaches among us. Cyprian tells us that the division and dissensions of the Christians was the cause of the persecutions in the primitive times; for said he, those evils had not come to the brethren, if the brethren had been united or animated into one. But I am sure that our Savior Christ said, 'By this shall all men know that ye are My disciples, if ye love one another'; and John, the disciple of love, said, 'By this ye shall know that you are translated from death to life, because you love the brethren.' See therefore that you love the brethren, and that *because* they are brethren. For a man may possibly love those who are good, yet not because they are good; for then he would love them better who are better, and those best who are best. If you love those that are good it is well; yet this may be for some self-concern, and your love then will be narrowed and your affections monopolized by some only of your own persuasion or relation. But if you love those who are good because they are good, this is better; for then you will love all who are good, though some of a different persuasion than you. Thus, O my sons, let your love be stated, continued, and increased towards men. But above all, be sure that you love Jesus for being Jesus. Love Christ for Himself, and let the only measure of your love be to know no measure."

Thus let the old man do and die, and as he lived by faith he shall die in the faith.

And as motives unto all these things, let the old man consider that:

In so doing he shall leave a sweet perfume behind him, and many shall bless God for him when he is dead.

There is enough in heaven to pay for all his pains here on earth.

He is not so weak but he is strong enough to sin; and shall he be strong to sin and not to serve?

It may be it was late before he came into God's work; and if you played away the morning of your age, will you not work the harder in the afternoon?

A Word to the Aged

God will accept both from youth and old age; from youth because it is the first, and from old age because it is the last, and from much weakness.

God's promise is very full; for He has promised and said, "Thou shalt come to thy grave in a full old age, and as a shock of corn cometh in his season" (Job 5:26). Yea, He has promised and said that "Those that are planted in the house of the Lord shall flourish in the courts of our God. They shall bring forth fruit in old age; they shall be fat and flourishing" (Psalm 92:13–14).

Thus they shall not be afraid to die, but shall say with that good man who was dying, "I have not so lived that I am afraid to die, but I have so learned Christ that I am not afraid to die."

Yea, and thus shall his old age be a good old age, and he shall "so number his days (it is not said his years, nor his months, nor his weeks, but days, for his life is so short that it is rather to be numbered by days than years, months, or weeks) that he shall apply his heart unto wisdom."

READY WHEN YOU ARE

Cecil B. DeMille's
Ten Commandments for Success

READY WHEN YOU ARE

Cecil B. DeMille's Ten Commandments for Success

By

Robert Hammond

www.newwaypress.com

READY WHEN YOU ARE: *Cecil B. DeMille's Ten Commandments for Success,* Copyright © 2012 by Robert Hammond. All rights reserved. Printed in the United States of America. This book may not be reproduced, in whole or in part, in any form or by any means electronic or mechanical, including photocopying, recording, or by any information storage and retrieval system now known or hereafter invented, without written permission of the publisher, New Way Press.

http://www.newwaypress.com

READY WHEN YOU ARE:
Cecil B. DeMille's Ten Commandments for Success
by Robert Hammond

ISBN-13: 978-0615673707
ISBN-10: 0615673708

Printed in the United States of America

ACKNOWLEDGEMENTS

Although I have written many books, this one came to me after years of researching the life and works of Cecil B. DeMille. *Ready When You Are* evolved as I came to know C.B and his life, his movies, his trials and his insight. I came to see that he was not only a genius in his art but a man who, despite some of his shortcomings, had great wisdom.

I thank the following people for contributing to this and my other DeMille projects: My wife, Lesa Hammond for her tireless support and encouragement; Casting Agent/Producer Gabrielle Evans-Fields and Producer/Manager Brandon Pender at Ithaca Entertainment Media Group for their continued efforts and bringing the *C.B. DeMille* biopic to the big screen; Professors Frank Montesonti, Helen Kantor, Ariane Simard at National

University for their early comments and suggestions on the *DeMille* script that led me to this obsessive exploration of the man who invented Hollywood; Colleagues Ken Burke at Mills College, Fay Guilian at University of Maryland, and Tynya Beverly at EDD University for providing forums to present Cecil B. DeMille and the Golden Age of Hollywood; Rob Gallagher, Terri Zinner, Daniel Gebretensai, Michael Beazel, Kurt St. Angelo, AJ Williams, Jim Wilkington, Ryan Gilmore, and everyone at Gallagher Literary for providing excellent reader notes on the original DeMille script; Robert Nudleman at the Hollywood Heritage Museum for sharing his knowledge and for helping to preserve the legend of DeMille; Brian Floyd and William V. Timmons for encouraging me to keep writing.

    A special thanks to the Los Angeles New Wave International Film Festival for acknowledging *C.B. DeMille* as Best Screenplay.

    And I am forever grateful to my mother, father, and son for believing in me and supporting my dreams through the years.

TABLE OF CONTENTS

Prologue 9
    How to make your dreams come true 9

Flashback 15
    Ready When You Are 15

C.B. DeMille 19
    The Man Who Invented Hollywood 19

The First Commandment 23
    Be Humble 23

The Second Commandment 25
    Be Amazed 25

The Third Commandment 29
    Be Ready 29

The Fourth Commandment 35
    Be Wise 35

The Fifth Commandment 41
    Be Steadfast 41

The Sixth Commandment 43
    Be Courageous 43

The Seventh Commandment 47
    Be Spectacular 47

The Eighth Commandment 49

Be Visionary	49
The Ninth Commandment	*57*
Be Truthful	57
The Tenth Commandment	*61*
Be Generous	61
Epilogue	*65*
That's a Wrap	65
Appendix A	*67*
The Bible as Blockbuster – The Influence of Cecil B. DeMille's Biblical Epics	67
Appendix B	*79*
Cecil DeMille also speaks	79
Appendix C	*89*
Motion Picture Directing	89
Appendix D	*119*
The Screen as a Religious Teacher	119
Appendix E	*125*
C.B. DeMille, An Epic Biopic of Cecil B. DeMille and the Creation of Hollywood	125
ABOUT THE AUTHOR	*129*
Robert Hammond	129

"Most of us serve our ideals by fits and starts. The person who makes a success of living is the one who sees his goal steadily and aims for it unswervingly. That is dedication."

~ C.B. DeMille

PROLOGUE

How to make your dreams come true

What if you discovered the lost memoirs of legendary director Cecil B. DeMille, hidden away in an old cellar, fifty years after his death? What if those pages revealed life-changing secrets that could transform the destiny of countless lives?

What would you want to know about Cecil B. DeMille? How did he break into Hollywood and begin making movies? Why did he persevere in spite of countless obstacles?

Fortunately for us, C.B. DeMille recorded many of his laws for living that have finally been revealed.

Before Hollywood was even a star on the map and movies were no more than novelties in the penny arcades, a certain man wanted to go out to California to make movies. Back then, movies were just cheap little machines you looked into for five cents where you could see a man taming a lion or a woman doing a strip tease. They called these arcade machines nickelodeons and that's what people thought about when you said you were going to make movies. So imagine what a person might think if somebody asked you to invest five thousand dollars in such a venture.

As you can imagine, back in 1913, five thousand dollars had a great deal more purchasing power than it does now. Adjusted for inflation, it would probably be like asking somebody today for five hundred thousand dollars or something like that. That's crazy.

This certain man asked his brother for five thousand dollars to invest in a twenty-five percent stake in his new motion picture production company. The other partners were a glove salesman and a New York theater producer. This certain man's brother was a successful playwright who thought that five thousand dollars would be lost foolishly if he invested in this venture. "What's twenty-five percent of nothing?" he asked. He answered his own question. "Nothing." And nothing is what he invested in the new company. And nothing is what he received back in dividends.

The certain man was Cecil B. DeMille, the legendary director who pioneered the Biblical epic and ushered in Hollywood's Golden Age. But have you ever heard of Cecil B. DeMille's brother, William DeMille? William was the one who was afraid to invest in Cecil's venture. How much do you think his five thousand dollar investment would be worth today? Who knows? Just to give you a little bit of an idea - one of Cecil B. DeMille's homes recently listed on the market for over twenty six million dollars. What do you think owning the rights to DeMille's seventy motion pictures might be worth today? How much would his share of Paramount Pictures be worth?

The other partners were theater producer Jesse Lasky and Jesse's brother-in-law Sam Goldfish. Sam was a glove salesman. He later changed his name to Goldwyn. They put up the remaining share in the business and were well rewarded for their efforts. You've heard of Goldwyn as in Metro-Goldwyn-Meyer or MGM. But that's another story.

Have you heard the story about the star of DeMille's first motion picture? Dusty Farnum was a successful theater actor when Cecil B. DeMille and Jesse Lasky approached him about starring in their film adaptation of The Squaw Man. DeMille offered Farnum the same deal he offered to his brother William. In exchange for starring in the film, DeMille promised to give Dusty Farnum 25 percent of the profits in the film. Dusty turned him down, saying, "No, I'll take my $250 a week. That's a sure thing I can count on."

Steven Spielberg credits C.B. DeMille with helping make his dreams come true. He fell in love with movies after watching Cecil B. DeMille's Academy Award-winning film, *The Greatest Show on Earth.* During his acceptance speech for the Golden Globe Cecil B. DeMille Lifetime Achievement Award in 2009, Spielberg described how C.B. DeMille's Academy Award winning film, The Greatest Show on Earth inspired him to make movies. He says he went home after seeing the film in 1952 and attempted to reenact the train wreck scene using his model train and an 8-millimeter home movie camera. Spielberg said, "I think what was on my mind when I was risking losing my Lionel train set was me thinking, 'Am I going to get away with this?' he recounted. "That anxiety has been haunting me throughout my entire movie career. Whenever I've tried to tell a risky story, whether it's about sharks or dinosaurs or about aliens or about history, I'll always be thinking, 'Am I going to get away with this?'" He says that C.B. DeMille showed him "how to put a lot of money up on the big screen and then make the studios pay for it."

DeMille's granddaughter, Cecilia de Mille Presley, said that she considers Spielberg, "The DeMille of today. Like Grandfather, he has consistently been able to capture vast audiences. He has had great commercial success without losing his personal vision or compromising his integrity."

Steven Spielberg is not the only person who has achieved his impossible dreams by following DeMille's strategies. I love reading biographies of men and women who have achieved extraordinary accomplishments, both in modern times and throughout history. As I have studied their lives, I have discovered that their successes, too, were realized by actions and attitudes that reflected DeMille's teachings, even though some may have never read his writings or seen his films. Oprah Winfrey, Billy Graham, Morgan Freeman, Tom Hanks, Martin Scorsese, Ron Howard, Edward G. Robinson, Gloria Swanson, and Charlton Heston were all great admirers of Cecil B. DeMille. They achieved their impossible dreams by practicing the very principles that DeMille reveals.

I discovered these principles of DeMille's success while I was working on my Master of Fine Arts in Creative Writing. I later wrote the novel and epic biopic screenplay, *C.B. DeMille* and the action/thriller *The DeMille Conspiracy*. What I didn't know at the time, having eight books already published, was that I had inadvertently applied many of DeMille's principles throughout the years. But by applying all ten Cecil B. DeMille's Commandments for Success, I see my dreams coming true more each day.

NOTE: The following pages contain excerpts from my novel and adapted screenplay, CB DeMille, the basis for the epic biopic about the life and work of the greatest showman on earth.

FLASHBACK

Ready When You Are

EGYPTIAN DESERT, 1955

C.B. DeMille sat in his director's chair, lowering the megaphone from his mouth. Desert winds swept sparkling desert sands against steep cliffs. The saffron sun scattered light and shadows across the shimmering dunes, revealing the Sphinx rising in the distance, and rows and rows of pyramids.

DeMille's daughter Ciddy, naturally pretty, her kind eyes shimmering with the natural wonder and imagination of a young girl, sat next to him. DeMille handed Ciddy his wooden cane, worn by time and use.

He turned to her slowly and asked, "Can you keep an eye on this?"

Ciddy took the cane in her hands and looked at it fondly then looking up at her father. "Oh, you think you don't need it anymore?" she asked.

"Something like that," he said with a twinkle in his eyes.

A young camera assistant kneeled before the camera and clapped the slate. "The Ten Commandments. Scene 70."

DeMille raised the megaphone back to his mouth. "Action!" he shouted.

Hundreds of horses and chariots galloped along the edge of the cliffs edging down the steep incline. Three cameramen caught the action from different angles.

The chariots descended to the bottom of the steep dunes in clouds of dust. DeMille stood to his feet. "Cut! That was fantastic. Perfect."

Moments later, DeMille looked over to Cameraman #1, raising the megaphone again. "Did you get that?"

Cameraman #1 pointed to what's left of his camera, half buried in the sand. "Sorry, C.B. The camera got trampled in the stampede."

DeMille looked to Cameraman #2. The cameraman looked at the front of the camera and wiped a big clod of dirt from the lens. He looked back at DeMille and shook his head.

DeMille jumped up and ran around frantically waving his arms at everybody, looking up to heaven, desperately pleading with God to save this precious shot. He lifted up his megaphone toward Cameraman #3. "Please tell me your camera is working."

Cameraman #3 smiled and gave DeMille a thumbs up.

"Ready when you are, C.B!"

C.B. DEMILLE

The Man Who Invented Hollywood

Cecil B. DeMille was born in 1881 to an Episcopal lay minister-turned dramatist and Jewish mother who ran a girl's school. After his father's death, when he was 12, DeMille attended military school. His mother's school for girls floundered and she started a theatrical booking agency. His brother, William became a successful Broadway playwright. C.B. DeMille struggled for the next twenty years, working as actor, barely making ends meet.

At the age of 33, DeMille made a decision that would change his life forever. In a fateful meeting with theater producer, Jesse Lasky and glove salesman Sam Goldfish (later Goldwyn), C.B. DeMille was offered the opportunity of a lifetime – to make motion pictures in California.

DeMille asked his brother, William to loan him the $5,000 he needed to get started, but William thought the venture was too risky. After all, in 1913, California was nothing more than desert and orange groves. Many people considered motion pictures to be a passing fad. DeMille's business partners decided to take a chance on him and advanced his portion of the initial investment. All DeMille needed was enough money to pay his way to California. His wife Constance supported him and offered to pawn the family silver. C.B. DeMille risked everything, temporarily leaving behind his wife and child in New York, to follow a dream. Because of his dream, what began in an old rented barn soon became the motion picture capital of the world.

    Soon after coming to Hollywood, DeMille fell into the temptations and self-destructive course to which so many creative people ultimately succumb. Rather than lose his business, his family, and his dream, DeMille sought wisdom and guidance by praying and studying the Bible.

    DeMille's subsequent spiritual awakening led to the making of the original silent version of *The Ten Commandments* in 1923. In the following years, DeMille's wisdom, success, and wealth increased beyond imagination. In terms of wealth, some have suggested that in today's dollars, he may well have been a "billionaire." In addition to his seventy films worth hundreds of millions of dollars in today's market, he owned hundreds of acres of prime Los Angeles real estate, and helped create Paramount Studios.

Business, religious, and political leaders of nations throughout the world honored DeMille and sought his advice. However, by the middle of his life, he began to violate the laws of living, its principles and strategies that he so wisely articulated; as he did, his success and happiness vanished. Fortunately, DeMille returned to the principles that made him so successful and achieved the greatest accomplishments of his life, including the restoration of his marriage, unlimited financial abundance, an Oscar award for Best Picture for his film *The Greatest Show on Earth*, and his crowning achievement, the making of the 1956 version of *The Ten Commandments* starring Charlton Heston.

THE FIRST COMMANDMENT

Be Humble

"Let the Divine Mind flow through your own mind, and you will be happier. I have found the greatest power in the world is the power of prayer."

"So, what do you think of Sam's idea?" Lasky asked DeMille.

Sam Goldfish grabbed two of the menus and handed them to DeMille and Lasky. He turned the first menu upside down and took out a pen. Goldfish said, "A verbal agreement isn't worth the paper it's written on."

Goldfish handed the menu and the pen to Lasky. Lasky scribbled something on the back of the menu and looked up. "The Jesse Lasky Feature Play Company. Good name since I'm the only one here with name recognition. And Sam, with his sales background will be in charge of distribution. That leaves you, C.B., as Director General, with total creative control."

Lasky handed the menu back to Goldfish, who read it to himself slowly and nodded approvingly. Goldfish handed the menu to DeMille.

DeMille read Lasky's scribbling and shook his head. "Total creative control. Sounds wonderful, except for one thing." He paused. "I know nothing about making pictures."

Goldfish slapped Lasky on the shoulder and the two men busted out laughing. Goldfish said, "Everything you need to know about making pictures you can learn in one day."

Begin with humility and your opportunities will be limitless.

THE SECOND COMMANDMENT

Be Amazed

"Creation is a drug I can't do without."

C.B. DeMille walked through the back lot of his studio where he witnessed a handler training one hundred white doves to fly across the stage in formation. In another section, he saw Mary Magdalene's leopard pace about a golden cage. A brilliantly plumaged Bird of Paradise sunned itself behind a wire netting under a giant arc light.

DeMille oversaw the shipping of seventy-five tons of props in fifteen trucks to the docks at San Pedro, where an entire passenger steamer waited to take cast, staff, and props across the water.

DeMille directed scenes by the Sea of Galilee filmed in Catalina and later, a scene with Julia as Martha at the tomb of Lazarus. He wept as he directed the scene of Jesus forgiving Mary Magdalene.

DeMille filmed a tremendous earthquake where dust swirled high by fierce winds.

———————————

Rabbi Magnin stood in front of DeMille at his desk. DeMille rose to greet him. "On behalf of B'Nai B'Rith organization, I congratulate you for doing such a fine work about a man of peace. God bless you, Mr. DeMille."

DeMille and Rabbi Magnin shook hands.

A Muslim Imam bowed with folded hands in front of DeMille, who returned the gesture. "Jesus is a central figure in our religion as well," said the Imam. "I pray that this work will bring people of all faiths together in peace and brotherhood."

"Thank you sir," said DeMille. That is my hope as well."

———————————

Searchlights arced across the night sky. Hundreds of fans, reporters and celebrities crowded into the historic Grauman's Chinese Theater, which opened with the premiere of *King of Kings,* and the film enjoyed wide public acclaim.

Rabbi Magnin stood next to DeMille as reporters and photographers gathered. He raised his voice so the crowd could hear him. "A great story is bound about a great man to bring about love and peace. Yet the One who has preached love and peace has been the center of such controversy that streams of blood have flowed to the sea. This story, free from any theology, will bring home to the world the true message that the great teacher taught through visual education."

Let your life continually be filled with a sense of amazement.

THE THIRD COMMANDMENT

Be Ready

"A picture is made a success not on a set but over the drawing board."

The set was an old west background with horses tied in front of a saloon. DeMille sat in front of the Barn in his director's chair, ordering around the cast and crew as they shot a scene from the film *Rose of the Rancho.*

Suddenly caravan of cars and trucks pulled up in front of the location. Jeanie Macpherson dressed in a long blue dress and fancy hat, barged onto the set with her own small cast and crew, interrupting the shot.

DeMille saw the commotion and jumped up from his director's seat. "Cut! Cut! Cut!"

Jeanie and her crew began setting up their own cameras and equipment. DeMille ran over and pushed her crew members back, knocking over one of their cameras. "What in heaven's name is going on here? Don't you know I'm in the middle of making a picture?" he yelled. "Now get out of here before I have you all thrown out. Who do you think you are?"

Jeanie looked DeMille in the eye and put her hands on her hips. A cigarette hung from her lips. "The name's Jeanie Macpherson and I'm the set manager for D.W. Griffith's picture. I'm afraid you'll have to move your equipment until we're done."

"OK. Wait here," said DeMille. He turned and marched into the Barn.

Moments later, DeMille came running out of the barn and chased Jeanie and her crew off the set with a shotgun.

Jeanie and her crewmembers jumped back in their vehicles and hightailed it out of there, leaving clouds of dust in their wake. DeMille fired the shotgun over their heads. Boom! Boom! Boom!

TWO DAYS LATER:

BANG! BANG! BANG!

DeMille sat at his desk writing in his red notebook. He ignored the person banging on the door as he continued writing. Jeanie barged in and stood in front of DeMille with her hands on her hips. "Mr. DeMille, I demand an apology."

DeMille sighed and continued writing in his notebook without acknowledging her.

"And I'll have you know that I'm not only a scenario writer and director, but I'm a great actress as well," she said. Jeanie lit up a cigarette before continuing. "As a matter of fact, I'm one of the greatest actresses you'll ever see. Even better than that over-rated tramp Norma Desmond."

DeMille glanced up at her briefly, and then continued with his work, without saying a word. Jeanie tossed her cigarette on the floor and stomped it out with her foot.

DeMille continued to ignore her.

"Well!" Jeanie stormed out in a huff.

Two weeks later, the glamorous Norma Desmond slowly descended a spiral staircase.

Jeanie quietly entered the set and stood in the wings.

"Cut!" DeMille shouted.

Norma walked up to DeMille and smiled.

"Good job, Norma," he said.

Norma exited as Henry Wilcoxen turned off the spotlights. DeMille headed towards his office and Jeanie followed him inside.

"I'm still waiting on that apology Mr. DeMille."

DeMille turns toward Jeanie, startled. Then he took his seat behind his desk. "I tell you what. I'll pay you twenty-five dollars a week to take dictation."

"Not only are you too stubborn to apologize for nearly killing me and my crew, but now you have the nerve to insult me." Jeanie stomped her foot and slammed her fists into her thighs. She suddenly straightened up and lit a cigarette, trying to regain her composure. "I tell you I won't stand for it. You let me walk out that door one more time and you'll regret it for the rest of your life."

Jeanie took a long drag from her cigarette. She exhaled as a tear slowly traced down her cheek. "I'm a wonderful actress, Mr. DeMille and I can write. I promise you're going to love me. Please, you've got to give me just one chance. Please, I'm begging you. I need this. Please."

Jeanie hung her head, sobbing desperate, pitiful tears.

DeMille sighed and rubbed his chin. "I'll pay you ten dollars for one day's work as an actress. Be here tomorrow morning at 8:00 a.m. And don't be late."

Jeanie looked up and wiped her eyes with her sleeve. "Ten bucks? You expect me to work a whole day for ten lousy bucks? What kind of girl do you think I am? Why I'm worth ten times that much!"

"Take it or leave it."

Jeanie took another drag from her cigarette and blew smoke rings. "Well, alright, I guess I'll take it. But consider this a big favor. You're going to realize that Jeanie Macpherson is worth her weight in gold. You'll see. I guarantee it." Then she skipped out of the room humming "Hooray for Hollywood".

DeMille chuckled and shook his head.

Understand the essential truth of always being ready for the unexpected opportunity.

THE FOURTH COMMANDMENT

Be Wise

"Give me any two pages of the Bible and I'll give you a picture."

Inside Paramount Studios later that day, DeMille sat at a conference table with Jeanie. He stood up and began pacing, hands clasped behind his back. "We've got to start looking at everything differently. We've got to think big. Biblical."

"What do you mean, C.B.?

DeMille stopped pacing. "I'm looking for the next big thing. I have a feeling that we are on the brink of a totally new kind of picture. I need to get a feel for what the public wants."

Jeanie laughed. "The public? What does the public know about making pictures?"

A newsboy hawked the morning headlines. "Extra! Extra! Read all about it. DeMille offers thousand dollar reward for movie idea." Dozens of people reached out to grab newspapers.

Two mailmen pulled bags of mail from the back of a mail truck behind Paramount Studios.

The mailmen poured out thousands of letters on DeMille's desk.

Later, DeMille and Jeanie sorted through the letters. DeMille opened a letter and read the contents aloud. "A man eating Boy Scout, a cowboy, and an aging Irishman team up to form a jazz trio in Cuba."

They both laughed. Jeanie opened another letter. "A bounty hunter goes on a fishing trip with a homicidal picture director."

DeMille rubbed his chin in thought. "Promising. But, no. What else we got?"

Later that evening, a haggard looking DeMille and Jeanie sat in front a much smaller stack of letters. The trashcan overflowed with crumpled pieces of paper. DeMille made a paper airplane with a discarded letter and tossed it across the room.

Jeanie picked up another envelope and opened it. As she read the letter, a big smile broke across her face. She stood up. "How about this one C.B.?" Jeanie held up the letter and read it aloud. "You cannot break the Ten Commandments – they will break you."

DeMille liked the idea. "The Ten Commandments?" he asked.

"The Ten Commandments!" Jeanie repeated.

"The Ten Commandments! Why of course. That's a wonderful idea."

DeMille stood in front of Paramount chief Adolph Zukor's desk with the letter in hand. "That's a horrible idea," said Zukor.

"How can you say that? We're talking about one of the greatest stories ever told."

Zukor got up from his seat, turned to the window behind him, and looked out toward the bustling city. He turned his back toward DeMille as he continued. "Old men wearing tablecloths and beards?" Zukor turned and walked around the desk toward DeMille. He placed his arm on

DeMille's shoulder. "Cecil, a picture like that would ruin us."

DeMille wasn't giving up without a fight. "Just think of it," he said. "We'll be the first studio to open and close the Red Sea."

"Maybe," said Zukor. "Or you'll be the first director to open and close Paramount." Zukor lit a cigar and paced around the room finally returning to his seat behind his desk. He took a puff of the cigar and blew smoke rings, imagining them as dollar signs. "So tell me," he began. How much is this baby going to cost me?"

DeMille smiled. "About a million dollars."

Zukor began choking on his own cigar and fell out of his chair. He stumbled to his feet. "What? A million dollars to make a lousy picture? You're crazy. Get out of my office! Now!"

DeMille broke out laughing.

Zukor wasn't laughing as he sat back down. "You think I'm kidding here?" he asked. "I mean it. Get out of here. And stay out until you come to your senses." Zukor paused for a moment, shaking his head in bewilderment. "You're killing me, Cecil. You're killing me!"

Zukor threw his cigar at DeMille, barely missing him. The cigar hit the wall and bounced into the wastepaper basket.

DeMille hustled out of Zukor's office as the wastepaper basket burst into flames.

A week later, C.B. DeMille stood in front of his desk, upon which were stacked about a hundred Bibles. Jeanie walked in and did a double take. DeMille looked up and smiled. "Ah. Just who I was looking for," he said. "Jeanie, make sure we get one of these to everyone on the payroll. And make it snappy. We've got a picture to make." DeMille handed Jeanie a stack of Bibles and gestured for her to get hopping.

Jeanie ambled down the hallway with her stack of Bibles and passed them out to everyone she saw.

Jess Lasky entered DeMille's office. "So you're really going through with this Ten Commandments project?" he asked.

"Give me two pages of the Bible and I'll give you a picture," DeMille said, as he handed Lasky a Bible. "Take it wherever you go and read it every day. The greatest source of material for motion pictures is the Bible, and almost any chapter in the Bible would serve as a basic idea for a motion picture."

Learn the importance of meditation and contemplation on the wisdom of the ages.

THE FIFTH COMMANDMENT

Be Steadfast

"Most of us serve our ideals by fits and starts. The person who makes a success of living is the one who sees his goal steadily and aims for it unswervingly. That is dedication."

The early sunlight was dim as DeMille entered the barn. A ruffle beneath his feet - He reached down and discovered...strewn all over the room. He picked up the unraveled film...Completely ruined. He fell to his knees.

DeMille stormed out of the barn, film in one hand, his gun in the other. "Who did this? Who did this?"

He crumpled the film in his fist. Lasky approached and puts his hand on DeMille's shoulder. "It's Zukor's boys from New York. We can't fight them," he said.

Goldfish said, "I tell you that Adolph Zukor thinks he owns the picture business. I never liked him and I always will."

DeMille balled his fist. "Success is our only option."

Inside the barn, DeMille huddled around a table with Dusty Farnum, Lasky, Goldfish, and young Henry Wilcoxen.

DeMille held up a handful of the ruined film. He looked around the room with curious contempt. "I refuse to be intimidated," he said as he tossed the film down on the table.

"What are we going to do?" Lasky asked.

DeMille looked Lasky in the eye sternly. "As God is my witness, we're going to make this picture. And then we're going to make another and another and another!"

DeMille stood to his feet and headed toward the door. He stopped and turned toward the men. "Now let's get back to work."

Discover the power of steadfast commitment.

THE SIXTH COMMANDMENT

Be Courageous

"Men will give their lives, gentlemen, to carry through. Nothing will stop them. They will do anything."

"I was shooting a scene in *The Little American* and we were firing a line of guns, supposedly French 75's. As they were using the real ones over in France we had to use imitations. In the middle of this scene the breech-block blew out of one of these guns and one man had a portion of his anatomy torn away, another had a great splinter go through his mouth and tear out his cheek; that whole gun crew was shot to pieces. But there wasn't one of those men that stopped acting. There wasn't a man on either side that turned to those fellows. They glanced at them as you would if it had been a real shell that struck and went on with their own guns until that scene was played through and the whistle blew. Then they went to these men.

"Men will give their lives, gentlemen, to carry through. Nothing will stop them. They will do anything."

During the filming of *The Ten Commandments*, DeMille directed a scene with hundreds of chariots heading toward the edge of the sand cliffs. The drivers came to a sudden halt, afraid to proceed. One of the stuntman, a well-built archer with a quiver of arrows on his back, approached DeMille. "The men are saying this scene is too dangerous," the Archer told DeMille. "We can't do it."

DeMille looked at him with disgust then turned to his young daughter Ciddy. "You want to show them how it's done, Ciddy?"

Moments later, Ciddy rode her pony up to the cliff and made the descent at breakneck speed and without injury. DeMille turned to the Archer with a disdainful smile. "Well, if a little girl like Ciddy can do it, why can't you?"

A few minutes later, hundreds of horsemen and chariot drivers rode down the steep slope, in a cloud of sand.

The dramatic scene concluded as the chariots descended to the bottom of the cliff in clouds of dust. DeMille jumped to his feet. "Cut! That was beautiful. Fantastic."

As the dust cleared, several stunt men writhed and groaned in the sand, covered in blood. Others limped away slowly.

Moments later, the Archer approached DeMille. "Mr. DeMille," he began, "my men are hurting. We need a break."

DeMille pointed to the setting sun. "See that?" he asked.

The Archer winced.

"The Israelites didn't complain about a few bumps and bruises," DeMille continued. "They knew the value of time. Now the sun is setting, we're losing daylight – you got two minutes." He glanced at his watch. "One minute and 55 seconds."

Later, DeMille stood next to the camera, yelling through his megaphone at the charioteers gathered below. "C'mon, you bunch of cowards. Let's make this look real!"

The Archer notched an arrow into his bow and fired it at DeMille's megaphone, the arrow embedding itself into the device just inches from DeMille's head. DeMille looked at arrow sticking out of the megaphone. "Action!"

Live courageously and do not give in to fear.

THE SEVENTH COMMANDMENT

Be Spectacular

"The way to make a film is to begin with an earthquake and work up to a climax."

The Exodus scene proceeded. Completely unrehearsed, the Jewish extras began singing in Hebrew the ancient Hebraic chants, tears streaming down their faces. They sang in unison, "Hear O Israel the Lord Our God, the Lord is One!" and DeMille burst into tears.

Ciddy reached for his hand. DeMille smiled at her. "Truly God is among us," he said.

Later, Egyptians in chariots chased the Israelites across the desert.

Horses stampeded and headed straight for the orchestra, leaving a heap of broken instruments and bruised musicians.

As the dust cleared, Zukor and his assistant Irving arrived on the set. They looked around in amazement. Zukor walked up to DeMille and shook his head. "Well, I didn't know the Israelites played instruments."

Inside DeMille's tent, Zukor waved a stack of papers in his hand. "You're killing me, Cecil! Look at this budget." He waved the stack of papers in front of DeMille.

"We ran into some unexpected situations," DeMille said.

Zukor read items from the budget. "Look. Medical bills - five thousand. Horses - ten thousand. Orchestra equipment - seventeen thousand. What's going on here?"

"We've only got a few more principle scenes to go. Then the second unit can finish up the rest," DeMille replied.

Zukor wasn't putting up with this. "You've got to cut the budget in half. Waive your guaranteed profit," he said, "or cut out the parting of the Red Sea."

DeMille held his ground. "What do you want here, the Five Commandments?"

The secret to great movies is the same principle for great relationships.

THE EIGHTH COMMANDMENT

Be Visionary

"I respect responsible criticism. What I deplore in many critics is not that they criticize, but that they do not see."

Inside DeMille's small apartment that night, Ciddy played with her wooden doll. Constance sat on the sofa beside her. "Look, mother. Dolly is a picture star." Ciddy manipulated the doll's hands and bounced the doll up and down on her knee. She pretended the doll was talking. "I am Cleopatra. Queen of the Nile."

Constance said, "That's very nice, dear. But you know that in pictures, the actors don't really speak out loud. They act."

Ciddy bounced the doll up and down on her knee and silently mouthed the words, "I am Cleopatra. Queen of the Nile."

DeMille entered the apartment and Ciddy tossed the doll down on the sofa. She jumped up and gave him a big hug. "Father! I'm teaching Dolly to be the star of a picture show."

Ciddy grabbed the doll and bounced her up and down in the air, pretending to make her talk. "I am Cleopatra. Queen of the Nile."

DeMille chuckled and clapped his hands in applause. "Oh, that's very good. Dolly is a very fine actress, my dear. In fact, I may just put her in one of my own pictures."

Ciddy clapped her hands. "Your own pictures?"

"Oh, Cecil," Constance interrupted. "Don't tease the girl like that."

"Who's teasing? That's what I've been waiting to tell you, my love. Something wonderful is happening," DeMille said.

Ciddy jumped up and down on the couch. "What is it, father?"

DeMille sat on the couch and motioned for Ciddy to come to him. Ciddy stopped jumping and took a climbed up on DeMille's lap.

"I'm going into the picture business," he said. "Everything is all worked out and I've been offered a job as Director General." He looked to Constance for her reaction.

Constance crossed her arms in front of her and looked away.

"I believe that this is going to be grand," DeMille said. DeMille slid Ciddy off his lap and stood to his feet. He paced the room as he spoke. "Imagine. What if you had this deep yearning to do something so profound and so far reaching that you could barely utter such a vision?"

"You're talking in riddles, Cecil," Constance replied. "Come on. Tell me what's going on?"

"I'm going into partnership with Jesse and his brother-in-law, a Mr. Goldman, or Goldfish, or something like that." DeMille took a seat on the sofa. Constance and Ciddy joined him.

"So Mr. Lasky and this other man you barely met are going to put up all the money?" Constance wasn't convinced.

"Yes, more or less. Well, something like that. They've agreed to cover my share of the initial investment until we make a profit.

Naturally, I'll need to pay my way to California. That's where we're going to set up shop."

"California? Who ever heard of making pictures in California? From what I hear there's nothing in California but desert and a few scattered orange groves."

"I know it all sounds crazy, but I have a vision. I need you to have faith in me. I promise not to let you down."

Constance grabbed DeMille and put her arms around him. She held him tightly, resting her head on his shoulder.

"I do have faith in you darling," she said.

Ciddy reached over and put her arms around both of them.

"So when should we pack our things?" Constance asked.

"But, I thought you understood," said DeMille.

Constance backed away from DeMille and stood to her feet. She put her hands on her hips. "Understood? Understood what? Cecil?"

DeMille rose and placed his hand on her shoulder. "Constance, my darling. You know that there's nothing that I care more about than you and Ciddy, and if I could take you both with me I would."

"What? You think you're going to go gallivanting across the continent and leave us here to fend for ourselves? I won't stand for it. No Cecil, please don't do this." Constance pounded DeMille's chest with her fists.

Ciddy began to cry. She jumped up and tugged on Constance's dress. "Stop it!" she cried.

Constance pushed Ciddy's hand away. "Ciddy, go to your room!"

DeMille tried to reassure Ciddy. "It's okay honey. Your mother and I are just talking about my trip."

Ciddy looked up at Constance. "I don't understand. Is father going away?"

"No, baby. Your father isn't going anywhere."

Constance turned and walked away. Ciddy grabbed DeMille's leg.

Constance brushed her hair as she prepared for bed. DeMille stood behind her with his hands in his pockets. "I was thinking that as soon as we turn our first profit, I would buy us a big house with a yard in the front and back. With trees."

"What do we need with a big house?" Constance asked. You know what the doctor said."

"What do doctors know? Anyway, we could adopt?"

Constance threw her brush at the mirror, breaking it. "Cecil. Will you stop? Please stop! Stop!"

Constance broke down crying. DeMille reached out and put his hand on her shoulder. "Darling, I'm sorry. You're right. It was a silly idea. I don't know anything about the picture business. I'll tell Jesse the deal is off. I'm sure we'll be fine right where we are."

Thunder echoed in the distance and hard rain crashed against the window. Water dripped from the ceiling onto the bed. DeMille grabbed a pan to catch the dripping rain.

The next day Constance gathered the family silver into a wooden case and handed it to DeMille. She said, "Do what you think is right and I will be with you."

DeMille held Constance in his arms. "Just don't forget about me while I'm gone," DeMille whispered in her ear.

Constance shook her head. "Don't be silly, darling," she said. How could I ever forget the one and only true love in my life?"

DeMille kissed Constance gently on the lips.

Ciddy entered the room rubbing her eyes. Ciddy looked up at DeMille with tears in her eyes. "You won't leave us will you?"

DeMille bent down and picked her up. She wrapped her little arms around his neck and kissed him on the cheek.

DeMille took a deep breath and let it out in a slow sigh. "I know that this is hard for you to understand right now, but please just trust me for now. I'll send for you and mother as soon as I can."

———————

DeMille entered the pawnshop and placed a silver set on the counter. Simpson, the middle-aged owner, counted out a stack of cash.

Outside train station - New York – day

DeMille stepped onto the train and waved goodbye to Constance and Ciddy. Constance wiped a tear from her eye and waved goodbye. The train whistle blew and the train chug, chug, chugged away from the station.

Ciddy ran after the train with her arms outstretched. "Don't leave us, Daddy!"

Constance ran out and grabbed Ciddy, picking her up in her arms. "Your father isn't leaving us, baby. He's just going to prepare a place for us. We'll be with him soon."

Ciddy turned toward the moving train and gave another little wave toward her father. "I love you!"

DeMille blew a soft kiss from the open door as the train headed down the track, leaving behind a wake of smoke, and then disappearing into the horizon.

Be true to your vision, even when others cannot see it. Imagine your impossible dreams coming true.

THE NINTH COMMANDMENT

Be Truthful

*"What I have crossed out I didn't like.
What I haven't crossed out I'm dissatisfied with."*

The ornate sign above the gated studio entrance read PARAMOUNT PICTURES.

Jeanie Macpherson sat at her desk typing on her Royal typewriter. Her fingers hunted and pecked the words: THE END. She ripped the paper out of the typewriter and placed it at the bottom of a manuscript. The cover page read "THE UNAFRAID."

She grabbed the script and ran to the adjacent office. The sign on the door read: CECIL B. DEMILLE, DIRECTOR-GENERAL. Jeanie dashed into DeMille's office and handed him the script.

DeMille took the script and sat back in his chair as he read the first few pages. He flipped through the script, skimming through the pages randomly until he came to the end. He picked up a red pencil and went back to the beginning marking up each page. "Come back in an hour," he said.

Jeanie stormed out of the office, slamming the door behind her.

One hour later, Jeanie stood back in front of DeMille's desk, nervously smoking a cigarette. "Well, what did you think?"

DeMille extended the script in Jeanie's direction and flipped through it so she could see the red markings on every page. "What I have crossed out I didn't like. What I haven't crossed out I'm dissatisfied with."

"What?"

"Quite frankly, Miss Macpherson, you write like a plumber. Nobody wants to see page after page of furniture descriptions. It reads more like a Sears Catalog than a motion picture scenario. I want to see a love story. Show me the heart. Show me the love." DeMille tossed the script at Jeanie and it fell apart, pages scattering in all directions. "Now go back and rewrite it with heart. And have it on my desk by noon tomorrow."

Jeanie gathered the scattered pages, crawling on her hands and knees across the floor. DeMille ignored her as he wrote in his notebook.

Inside Jeanie's office that night, Jeanie clickity clacked on the typewriter. The clock on the wall chimed midnight, then 2:00 a.m., then 4:00 a.m. DeMille entered Jeanie's office and saw her sleeping on the floor. He tenderly lifted her to the sofa and her shoe fell off. He laid his coat across Jeanie's shoulders as she slept.

Always tell the truth, no matter how difficult it may be.

THE TENTH COMMANDMENT

Be Generous

"I hoped those who saw <u>The Ten Commandments</u> would not only be filled with the sight of a big spectacle but filled with the spirit of truth."

HOLLYWOOD, CA 1923

That night the Egyptian Theatre marquee read:

CECIL B. DEMILLE'S
THE TEN COMMANDMENTS
WRITTEN BY JEANIE MACPHERSON

Big stars, reporters, and VIP's gathered for the premiere. DeMille exited a limousine with Constance and Ciddy by his side. Reporters and photographers crowded the scene. Cameras flashed.

Inside the Egyptian Theater, the Red Sea parted in glorious Technicolor®.

HOLLYWOOD, 1946

DeMille sat in his office, writing in his notebook. Jeanie approached DeMille, looking tired and gaunt. DeMille stood up and moved from behind his desk to greet her. "Jeanie. Please sit down." He guided her to the couch. "May I get you something? Some water?"

"Water would be nice," she said.

DeMille poured Jeanie a glass of water and handed it to her. He sat on the couch next to her.

Jeanie took a sip of the water and set it down on the table. She laid her head on DeMille's shoulder and began sobbing uncontrollably. DeMille comforted her. "There, there," he said. "It's alright." He stroked her hair.

"No, C.B. It's not alright." She wept. "The doc says it's cancer."

DeMille lowered his head. "Dear God," he whispered. "Is there anything I can do to help? Do you need money?"

Jeanie shook her head as she struggled to her feet. DeMille helped her up. Jeanie walked away. She stopped and turned toward DeMille. She looked at him with longing and remembrance. "Forget about me, C.B. Go take care of your wife." She walked out of the office.

HOLLYWOOD, CA 1955

An aging actor Edward G. Robinson, stood in front of DeMille dressed in Egyptian robes for the role of Dathan. "I thought I'd never work again," said Robinson. "But you took a chance and gave me break. I'll never forget you." Robinson wept as DeMille gave him a big bear hug, slapping him on the back.

"Let's pray those days are behind us," said DeMille.

**Give and it shall be given unto you.
The secret of great wealth is in great giving.**

EPILOGUE

That's a Wrap

**C.B. DeMille's
Ten Commandments for Success**

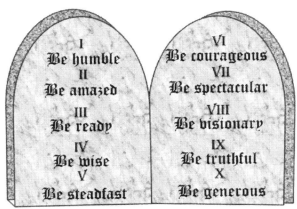

I Be humble
II Be amazed
III Be ready
IV Be wise
V Be steadfast
VI Be courageous
VII Be spectacular
VIII Be visionary
IX Be truthful
X Be generous

Ready When You Are: C.B. DeMille's Ten Commandments for Success combines years of research from various sources including excerpts from my forthcoming novel and screenplay, *C.B. DeMille*.

As you learned about the life and work of Cecil B. DeMille, I hope that you were entertained and enlightened. As you apply these principles to your own life, you will discover that you can make your dreams come true, no matter what the critics say. The only limitations are the ones you set for yourself.

Realize that, like gravity, these Ten Commandments for Success are universal, interconnected principles, not bound by any one religion or culture or time. These principles are free for everyone. Feel free to share them with anybody and everybody. Cherish these principles in your heart and live them out in your life. Your dreams will come true.

The following pages include a series of articles, including a scholarly paper on the influence of DeMille's Biblical epics (Appendix A), along with articles about making movies written by C.B. DeMille himself (Appendices C and D). You will also find more information about the original screenplay, *C.B. DeMille*. (Appendix E).

APPENDIX A

The Bible as Blockbuster – The Influence of Cecil B. DeMille's Biblical Epics

By Robert Hammond

"Give me two pages from the Bible, and I'll give you a motion picture" ~ *Cecil B. De Mille*

Cecil B. DeMille was a born showman, one of the most prolific and successful directors of all time, and the man who was most responsible for turning Hollywood into the world's film capitol. As the creative force behind Paramount Studios, DeMille "handled every existing film genre and formulated some that never existed before" (Katz, 366), most notably the Biblical epic.

In 1923, Hollywood was on the brink of moral implosion, rocked with scandals like the murder of William Desmond Taylor and Fatty Arbuckle's arrest for child rape and manslaughter. America was still reeling from the devastation of World War I, mourning the loss of its sons in the War to End All Wars. Cecil B. DeMille, having already made forty-one motion pictures brought forth his original version of *The Ten Commandments*, a spectacular event unlike any other film before its time.

In preparation for the filming of *The Ten Commandments* DeMille sent a copy of the Bible to every employee with the words, "As I intend to film practically the entire book of Exodus…the Bible should never be away from you. Place it on your desk, and when you travel, stick in your briefcase. Make reading it a daily habit." (Higham, 111-114).

Jeanie Macpherson, who developed the story into two parts, wrote the screenplay. The first part was a retelling of the story of the Exodus, where Moses led the children of Israel from the oppression of Egyptian slavery to the edge of the Promised Land, culminating in the parting of the Red Sea and the giving of the stone tablets containing Ten Commandments from Moses' encounter with God on Mt. Sinai. The second part was a contemporary Cain and Abel story about two sons of an ultra-religious mother, both of whom fall in love with the same woman. The youngest son rejects the Commandments and sets out to break every one of them, while the eldest son strives to live according to God's law. In a memorandum to DeMille, Macpherson wrote:

> As the sins of Pharaoh and his horde of horsemen are avenged by the down-crashing waves of the Red Sea, which parted to let the Children of Israel, with their clear faith, pass through, so does the emotional Red Sea engulf our modern [antagonist] Dan McTavish, who has attempted to raise his puny voice against immutable laws. (109-110).

DeMille filmed *The Ten Commandments* on the sand dunes of Guadalupe, California, using a literal "cast of thousands," including 600 chariots, and hundreds of trained animals. For many people this was the first time they had seen the Bible come to life. With limited access to movie theaters in rural areas, churches screened the film across sheets during special services and social events. The parting of the Red Sea was the greatest film spectacle the world had ever seen.

In 1926 DeMille handed Jeanie the worn family Bible, which his father had used, and gave her what he, referred to as "the most important assignment of her life." He instructed her to follow the great drama of the Gospels to the letter, patently rejecting her idea to frame it with a modern counterbalance. As he did during the production of *The Ten Commandments*, DeMille sent copies of the Bible to every member of his staff, ordering them to memorize every word of the Gospels, and holding daily Bible studies. His research team "explored twenty-five hundred volumes and fifty thousand feet of documentary film [condensing them]...for Jeanie and her own assistants to examine." The cameraman Peverell Marley was instructed to study hundreds of biblical paintings, particularly those by Gustave Dore and Rubens. (Higham, 160-161).

On August 24, 1926, the first day of shooting, DeMille invited members of the clergy to offer their blessings. In his introductory remarks, he proclaimed:

> We are on the eve of a very vital thing to the world. So far as I know, it is the first time in history that a group such as this has gathered informally to bless an undertaking. In this little group are represented the great religions of the world, all centered on one point – the life, philosophy, and teachings of a great man. No matter whether you believe God descended to mortality or mortality rose to Divinity – His life is an open book – no matter what belief, everyone believes this One man has done a great thing for humanity. We want to give His Work renewed force and vigor and spread it to all parts of the world in order that His motives

and sincerity may be understood. We have asked representatives of each faith to give us their good thoughts that the right message be given. Thought means so much – hold for us the right thought to help us do our bit toward spreading the great gospel that this great man taught.

Rabbi Magnin of the Jewish organization B'Nai B'Rith, congratulated DeMille on the production, stating:

> A great story is bound about a great man to bring about love and peace. Yet this one who has preached love and peace has been the center of such controversy that streams of blood have flowed to the sea…This story free from any theology, will bring home to the world the true message that the great teacher taught through visual education.

Grauman's Chinese Theater opened with the premiere of *King of Kings* and the film enjoyed wide public acclaim.

Billy Graham acknowledges *King of Kings* as a profound influence, calling DeMille "a prophet in celluloid". Graham's daughter Anne Graham Lotz credits the film as being a catalyst for her childhood conversion to Christianity.

ABC continues to broadcast the film every year during the Passover week to consistently high ratings (Mitchell, 6).

In the filmed introduction to the 1956 version of *The Ten Commandments* DeMille stated, "The theme of this picture is whether men are to be ruled by God's law or whether they are to be ruled by the whims of a dictator like Rameses. Are men the property of the state or are they free souls under God?"

Many critics found DeMille's moralizing obvious and heavy-handed. Robert S. Birchard, in his article, "Cecil B. DeMille Vs. The Critics," argues that DeMille's anti-Communist politics played a part in his critical response, noting, "it simply wasn't fashionable for the political left to acknowledge Cecil b. DeMille as anything more than a bourgeois capitalist vulgarian." This despite the fact that DeMille's "The Volga

Boatman" was well received in the U.S.S. R. as being sympathetic to the Russian Revolution.

In his autobiography, DeMille wrote, "I respect responsible criticism. What I deplore in many critics is not that they criticize, but that they do not see."

In a memo to Louis B. Mayer, movie mogul David O. Selznick confessed:

> However much I may dislike some of his [DeMille's] pictures from an audience standpoint, it would be very silly of me, as a producer of commercial motion pictures, to demean for an instant his unparalleled skill as a maker of mass entertainment, or the knowing and sure hand with which he manufactures his successful assaults upon a world audience that is increasingly indifferent if not immune to the work of his inferiors. As both professionally and personally he has in many ways demonstrated himself to be a man of sensitivity and taste, it is impossible to

believe that the blatancy of his style is due to anything but a most artful and deliberate and knowing technique of appeal to the common denominator of public taste. He must be saluted by any but hypocritical or envious members of the picture business (Behlmer, 400).

DeMille's 1956 remake of the *Ten Commandments* was the largest and grandest motion picture made up until that time, with 1200 storyboards, a 308-page script and 70 speaking parts. Historian Sumiko Higashi called DeMille's remake of *The Ten Commandments* an "antimodernist historical film for today's postmodern culture."

DeMille gave formerly blacklisted actor Edward G. Robinson a new start, essentially rescuing his career. In his autobiography, "All My Yesterdays" Robinson wrote, "Cecil B. DeMille returned me to films. Cecil B. DeMille restored my self-respect. DeMille also gave immigrant Ayn Rand a part as an extra to give her a hand in being established.

DeMille employed more women behind-the-scenes in well-paid professional positions than any other filmmaker, including writer-scenarist, Jeanie Macpherson, film editor, Anne Bauchens, and aide de camp, Gladys Rosson. He was also explicit in his depiction of the mixed-race relationship between Moses played by Charlton Heston and the Ethiopian princess played by black actress, Esther Brown (Mitchell 4).

DeMille pioneered the Biblical epic. *The Ten Commandments* (1956) was the most successful and best-known film of its era. During the 1950's and early 60's many of the stories from the Old Testament were put on the big screen and were among the highest grossing films of that period. Biblical epics such as *David and Bathsheba* (1951), *Solomon and Sheba* (1959), *David and Goliath* (1960), and *Sodom and Gomorrah* (1963), dominated the box office.

The New Testament did not present as much romance and physical action as many of the Old Testament stories, and neither DeMille's *King of Kings* nor director George Stevens' *The Greatest Story Ever Told* (1967) received as much critical or box office success. However, several fictional stories involving the life of Christ including *The Robe* (1953), *Quo Vadis* (1951), and *Ben Hur* (1959) were hugely successful. In 1966, Pier Paolo Pasolini filmed *The Gospel According to Matthew* in Southern Italy with nonprofessional actors and, despite the Marxist director's admitted atheism, the Pope praised the film for its scriptural accuracy.

During the '70s and '80's true Biblical epics fell out of fashion due to the change in social climate, although some controversial films such as the musical *Jesus Christ Superstar* (1973), the parody *The Life of Brian* (1979), and Scorcese's *The Last Temptation of Christ* (1988) were financially successful. In 2004, Mel Gibson's independently produced *The Passion of the Christ* made film history as one of the highest-grossing films of all time. *The Passion of the Christ* revived Hollywood's interest in the Biblical epic and several studios have now dedicated divisions to producing faith-based films. However, Cecil B. DeMille deserves credit for creation of Biblical epic as a genre that has had a major effect upon the film industry and millions of individual's lives.

Behlmer, R. (Ed.). Memo from David O. Selznick. New York: The Viking Press. (1972).

Birchard, Robert, S. Cecil B. DeMille Vs. The Critics. In *L'Eredita DeMille (The DeMille Legacy)* Pordenone: Edizione Biblioteca dell'immagine. 1991.

Braudy, Leo and Cohen, Marshall. (Ed.). Film Theory and Criticism 6th Edition. Oxford: 2004.

Higashi, S. Cecil B. DeMille and the American Culture: The Silent Era. University of California Press. Berkeley: 1994

Higham, C. Cecil B. DeMille. New York: Charles Scribner's Sons, 1973.

Katz, Ephraim. The Film Encyclopedia, 5th Edition. New York: Harper Collins, 2005.

Mitchell, Lisa. Legacy. www.cecilbdemille.com/legacy.html

APPENDIX B

Cecil DeMille also speaks

By Peter Milne (1922)

In which it is noted that the more famous DeMille, besides employing the method of production described by his brother, places unusual faith in the intelligence of his actors and actresses. "Never show them HOW but tell them WHAT" is his formula. A case where an actor insisted on being shown.

Mention of one of the DeMilles immediately brings to mind the other. Cecil and William are as easy to say in one breath as Anthony and Cleopatra, Nip and Tuck and Mutt and Jeff.

Cecil B. DeMille is one of the few directors of today whose name carries a picture to the financial success that greets a picture bearing the name of a great star. It appears that he first rode to national fame when he inaugurated a series of pictures bearing such mandatory and interrogatory titles as *Don't Change Your Husband* and *Why Change Your Wife?*

But long before this he was cutting wide swaths in the old fashioned method of directing by doing his work in a distinctly individual and better way. Pictures such as *The Golden Chance* and the first edition of *The Squaw Man* stamped him as considerably more of an artist than the earlier pioneers in the art of directing.

Cecil DeMille was, perhaps, the first director to use the method of producing his pictures in continuity, as outlined by his brother in the previous chapter. Perhaps this is the reason that he early secured such superior results to those achieved by the general run of directors in the early days.

Or perhaps on the other hand it is his ability to handle actors and actresses so as to get the very utmost from their efforts. For Mr. DeMille claims that one of the primal rules of directing is "never tell an actor how to play a scene."

On this axiom, he states, lies the secret of achieving real characterization and absolute naturalness on the screen.

This may appear to be a perfectly natural conclusion to some readers. An actor of ability knows his business and therefore knows how to develop a true characterization. All he needs is a few words from the director as regards the timing of his transition from one emotion to another.

This is becoming more and more true as the art of picture production develops but the time is easily recalled when directors boasted that they acted out every part of the picture so that their casts might secure the proper grasp of the story.

I remember very well one director, a big man in his day but who has since sunk to oblivion as far as picture production goes, who used to take great delight in showing his players how to play certain scenes.

After a few preliminary rehearsals, he would become disgusted or pretend to become disgusted, with the efforts of his cast and thereupon he would act out each and every role for the cast's benefit. It was rather ridiculous to see him affecting the coy mannerisms of an ingénue, then jumping quickly into the role of the hero and from there to the contrasting part of the villain. He would even perform the butler with pompous dignity for the benefit of the extra who was playing the part.

But what effect did all this play on the director's part have on the on-looking cast? The director's personality and individual mannerisms were displayed in every role. Thereafter the actors endeavored to imitate him not to enact their parts. The hero merely gave an imitation of the director giving an imitation of the hero. The ingénue gave an imitation of the director imitating the ingénue. And so on through all the parts.

The results, it need hardly be pointed out, were not natural. In the end all the players gave bad imitations of the director. On top of this they endeavored to effect his mannerism and tricks of expression. As a consequence there was absolutely nothing distinctive about the completed picture. It was the director's and no one else's. The director, being conceited to a great degree, was naturally delighted with the result. But he was the only one delighted with it as is testified by the fact that he is not in the art today.

This method has gradually been forced out of the studio. There are few directors who insist on acting every part out nowadays. There are some left but not many. A few more years and they will all disappear and then we will have still better pictures.

Mr. DeMille evidently believed that a good many directors of the present day still adhere to the old fashioned method. It is to be hoped that he isn't altogether right.

"Too many directors," he says, "consider it their duty to show an actor just how to play every scene in the picture. This type of director insists on acting out every role and demands that his cast shall mimic his action before the camera. The results are woefully wooden, unnatural and characterless.

"In the perfect photoplay each character must be distinctly itself. It must be sharply differentiated from all other characters in that particular play. This result can only be achieved by permitting each actor or actress to work out his or her own interpretation of a role.

"If I show an actor how to pick up a paper or a book in a scene he will consciously strive to imitate my actions. Now, what may be perfectly natural for me may be unnatural and awkward for him. At the best his attempt to copy my model will be but a poor reproduction of Cecil B. DeMille on the screen. If I carried that program through with respect to each player I would have just as many weak versions of Cecil B. DeMille as there are characters in the play.

"If, on the other hand, I explain to the actor what the action of the scene is and what idea or emotion I want him to convey to the spectator and then permit him to work out his own interpretation of the scene I have a distinctive, natural and far more powerful piece of work from that actor. I assume that every actor is better at creating than mimicking me.

"My task comes in my effort to perfect his interpretation by helpful criticism and suggestion but not by example.

"Before beginning actual production on a picture I make it a rule to call together the entire cast and the technical staff. At this meeting, I tell them the story with all the detail of characterization and atmosphere that I am capable of putting into it. I do not read them the continuity scene by scene. I try to make them see and feel the story and the characters and, as everyone in the production arts knows, the straight reading of a continuity is an uninteresting and tedious proposition.

"So when the cameras actually start to turn, each member of the cast has his or her own characterization and its relationship to the others well in mind.

"At the beginning of each scene I sketch out verbally what the action of the scene is to convey to picture audiences. Then comes a rehearsal and often many rehearsals before it is actually filmed. But through all these rehearsals I make a point of never showing anyone how to do a thing. If an actor does something badly or awkwardly, I try to locate the cause of the awkwardness and remedy that. By way of example, the scene may call for an actor to be seated at a desk thoughtfully smoking a pipe. Perhaps the actor may handle the pipe like an amateur. Inquiry may uncover the fact that he is far more at home smoking a cigar. Thereupon the cigar is supplied and the scene proceeds smoothly.

"A little thing, to be sure, but between the pipe and the cigar lies the difference between a natural and an unnatural performance.

"No actor worthy of his calling should have to be shown how to play a scene. He may have to be coached; that is part of the director's task. But it is no part of the director's duties to furnish the acting model for any or every character in the play. I firmly believe that attempts on the part of the directors to show actors how to do certain things will inevitably result in bad performances and consequent damage to the quality of the finished production."

C.B. DeMille's comments are very interesting. It is to be supposed that he does not give copies of the picture continuity to his players that they may thoroughly acquaint themselves with the parts they are to play before actual production work begins. Today the majority of directors like to do this.

However, as DeMille says, "I tell the story with all the detail of characterization and atmosphere that I am capable of putting into it." This appears to be an admirable course to pursue. Given the continuity an actor may get quite the wrong idea of the role he is to play. Listening to his director sketch the story, including in it his ideas as to its development, must of necessity give the actor a clear idea of his work and an idea more coinciding with that of the director's. Thus it might appear that misunderstanding and argument are well disposed of.

On the other hand, C.B. DeMille is fortunate in having players of general intelligence and ability to deal with. Look over any of the casts he has employed in his recent productions, *The Affairs of Anatol* for example, and you will discover that there is hardly an unknown in the entire cast.

It is amusing to consider what Mr. DeMille would have done if he had had the task of producing *Cappy Ricks*, a picture made by one of the directors that Mr. DeMille developed, Tom Forman. There was the role of a Swedish sea captain, humorously called "All-Hands-and-Feet" in this picture.

An old prizefighter was selected to play the role. He looked the part to perfection. But the scenario called for the star, Thomas Meighan, to engage in a fight with him and knock him out. The ancient fighter was perfectly agreeable for the fight, in fact, he battered his opponent considerably but when it came time for him to be knocked out he just wouldn't fall down.

The scene was tried over and over again and each time when it came to the psychological moment "All Hands-and-Feet" positively refused to fall down on the deck after Mr. Meighan had delivered a blow on the chin.

"Go down! Down!" Mr. Forman kept repeating wrathfully.

"Down? Down?" queried the one time prizefighter, "I no understand what you say."

Eventually Mr. Forman had to submit to the ignominy of allowing Mr. Meighan to land on his chin and drop him on the deck.

A broad grin crept over the benign countenance of "All-Hands-and-Feet" as he said, "Ah, I never bane knocked down, I see what you mean. I try to fall next time."

Mr. Forman and Mr. Meighan started a movement to back "All-Hands-and-Feet" for the championship of the world. But when their subject heard of it he mysteriously disappeared. Possibly he didn't want to be taught what "down" meant in a serious way.

Peter Milne, "Cecil DeMille Also Speaks," in "Motion Picture Directing," (1922, New York: Falk Publishing Co., Inc.), pages 47-56.

APPENDIX C

Motion Picture Directing

By Cecil B. DeMille

President DeMille Studios,
Hollywood, California

This paper was originally presented before the Graduate School of Business Administration of Harvard University, April 26, 1927.

A motion picture director in many respects occupies a position analogous to the leader of an orchestra. The leader has to wave a baton in order to get the right tempo. He has to see that the bassoon does not come in while the violin is playing its solo. Likewise a motion picture director has to hold together all the departments, he has to see that they all function on time, and that everything meets on the little set where the camera is going to turn for a few minutes.

I will review first the period of preparation to bring about that moment. There are three classes of directors. There is the director who has been sufficient of a success in the past to have the confidence of his institution and is allowed to choose more or less his own subject. There is the director who is sent for and handed a manuscript and told "This is what you shoot." He takes that manuscript, works on it, and says, "I suggest the following changes." Then there is the director to whom you say, "Take this manuscript and shoot it just the way it is written and don't change anything."

In the first place, as I know more about the first class, I will discuss that as a basis. The first thing is the idea. What idea are you going to produce? The sales department will always name to you the last success, whatever it was, and say, "Produce something like that because it was a success." Had you named that idea to the sales department before it was a success they would have thrown their hands up in horror and would have said, "But nobody wants to see that." This has been my experience in blazing a trail practically from the beginning of pictures, that nobody was in sympathy with the subject I wanted to do until after it was a success. Then I was a great hero. But until that point I was the national villain, and if I use "'I" a good deal, I apologize for it in advance. I am speaking editorially.

To make my point a little clearer let us consider *The King of Kings*. At a time when everybody was producing melodrama, when such pictures as *Crime* and *Broadway* and *The Spider* were intriguing the public, I felt that the world was ready for the life of Christ. When I suggested it, we almost had to artificially resuscitate the financial department. They said, "No; what they want is melodrama." That is the time, however, to do the other thing.

I made a picture recently called *The Volga Boatman*. When I suggested it to the financial department they. said, "But nobody is interested in Russian peasants." After the picture was a success they said, "There, we told you." That is the attitude, and it always will be, of the sales department.

The production department acts more or less as a bouncer between the director, who has his vision, and the financial department, who sometimes lack it. So, the subject is selected.

Then comes the matter of the treatment, at least as to whether the subject is big enough to make what we call a super-special, that is, a picture that is road showed or released separately or whether the subject is not sufficiently big in quality, so that it should be a program picture.

When that point is decided the amount of money to be expended comes next, whether the idea is big enough to carry $50,000, $100,000, $300,000, $500,000, or $1,000,000, as the case may be. In the case of *The King of Kings* the cost was $2,500,000. That seemed a ridiculous amount of money to expend on an idea that the financial department were sure could not be successful.

That is why the director has gray hairs, because he is the fellow who dreams, and he has to make his dreams come true. That is the advantage he has over most dreamers. He has no choice. If he does not make them come true he is like the general who does not take his objective, and you know what happens to generals who don't.

You are given a scenario writer. Your first treatment resembles the plan of a house. You do not sit down and have a writer write a scenario. You draft a treatment, that is, a plan. You look for a foundation on which to stand your story.

Has it a theme? Is it episodic? Is it dramatic? The treatment may be done over and over again but the wise director will never let his manuscript go to continuity form until he has that treatment. In other words, it is as if you were going to build a house and the architect said, "I have a magnificent roof and some lovely walls," and you said, "What are you going to stand it on?"

He would say, "I don't know, but the roof is beautiful." That is the danger of the green director or the green writer. They are blinded by the beauty of the walls and the roof, but if there is not a great dramatic foundation underneath your structure it will not stand, no matter how beautifully played it is and no matter how beautifully directed.

If your treatment is as strong as you can make it, then comes your continuity. Continuity is the scene for scene scenario. What is generally known as a scenario is the continuity. It is equivalent to the dialogue of a play. The playwright does not start out to write beautiful dialogue until he has a structure on which to hang it. So the first treatment is the structure on which you hang the continuity, which is the written sequence of scene.

The continuity comes to the director and goes back to the writer again and again and again, and a great deal of money goes into that going back, and back, and back. The wise business department knows that where a picture is made or lost is over the desk. You cannot hand a director a poor story or a poor scenario without good drama. No matter what ingredients he may use, he cannot give you a good picture unless he has the essentials. You may have a beautiful cannon but if the powder is no good it will not throw the balls very far no matter how fine a sighter the gunner may be or what fine soldiers may be handling the machine. If the powder is wrong, you are out of luck. So it is with the story. Therefore, you take time over, and over, and over again to look for weakness from every angle, in every scene.

Take a scene where a man comes in, sits down, and picks up the telephone. The first-class director has the man come in, sit down, and pick up the telephone. Your highest class director says, "How on earth can I make that interesting, so it will hold an audience for just a second, so that it is not just a man coming in, sitting down and picking up a telephone? What twist can I give that to make a little smile come to the audience? If merely the cord of the telephone catches in the drawer that little incident means a lot because the audience thought they were going to be bored and then they say, Oh! That little exclamation, Oh! has a great psychological effect." That is the way every scene should be worked out in the mind of the director.

Then we see that the scenario is right, which it seldom is, but we take that for granted.

Then he calls in the art director. The term art director is sometimes a bit misleading. He is the man who designs or has designed the sets. He is the head of that department. If the story is modern, again comes the point of "How can we make this a little more interesting, a little different from the last picture made?" He says, "Well, this series is a short series. If it isn't of any particular value pictorially, we have a set already that was used in such and such a picture." The director says, "Can that be disguised? - Can you change that door into a window so it will not be recognized as the set that was used in the last picture?" The art director says he can or cannot, as the case may be.

We will say we have a great scene called for,- the vision of temporal power in *The King of Kings*, which Satan shows to Jesus, where the power of the world is depicted. That is the proposition that is put up to the director,- how to depict the power of the world, how to show it, how to do it. That is the kind of proposition the director gets. He has his art director, his technical man, his trick man, stunt man, miniature man, and glass man.

For instance, in the scene I just mentioned, the vision of temporal power, we changed the temple into a vision of Rome and, because it is an imaginative thing, it was necessary to show Rome even more magnificent than it was, in other words, a hundred Romes piled one on top of another. That would be impossible to accomplish if you went out and built it. It would take as long and cost a good deal more to build Rome, because wages are higher now than they were then. You take your miniature man, your glass man, your art director, your carpenter, and you say you are going to use a foreground of 500 or 1000 feet in this. We will build this set for 500 feet, the actual set. From that point on we make a miniature which is matched by very clever camera work to the real set. Then we have glass on which we paint, clearing the glass to show the real set and the miniature, and on top of that, because it is supposedly far in the background, we have painted by the finest artist we can get, the imaginary Rome. The real thing is in the foreground, the miniature just above it showing the roofs of the great city of Rome, cleverly blended as to what we have built, and then this glass picture in front of that but really giving the effect of a far-distant horizon. Then the camera is set back a certain distance. In that way, these great scenes are made possible.

Do not get the idea that this is not an expensive process. The making of the miniature and the matching must be very carefully done because it must not be detected. Some of you may have seen the picture called *The Ten Commandments*. In that we were given the proposition of opening and closing the Red Sea. That is what the director was told to do. He can't ask how because nobody can tell him. Nobody had opened and closed the Red Sea before except on one memorable occasion, but we nevertheless had to duplicate that. That was done with 14 exposures on the film. I am not going to dwell too much on these technical points but I want to give you a little idea of what I mean.

There were 14 pictures or exposures on the opening and closing of the Red Sea. That was a mixture of the real sea and very clever motion picture trick work. The wave which engulfed Pharaoh's army was obtained by building two tanks holding 60,000 gallons of water each, designed to drop at the same moment onto a large curved piece of steel so that when it threw this wave into an enormous curve, the two things met at the top, and we got a wave in that way that was enormous. The camera was almost underneath it. That is before you start in with your people at all.

This probably sounds like Chinese music to you, but it is impossible to give you in three-quarters of an hour the mechanical working of the trick department of a motion picture studio. The art director, however, in conference with you, covers these points in connection with scenes which require this treatment.

Then comes the costume department, and you discuss the matter of the types of clothes, and so forth. If it is a costume picture the research department must start months before, because, for instance in *The King of Kings*, you cannot take Renaissance paintings and say, "Let us find out what the costumes were there." If you recall Rembrandt's painting of Pharaoh's daughter finding Moses in the bulrushes, she is clad in a long-waisted Elizabethan gown, and the page holding back the bulrushes is in tights with velvet trunks and a red hat with a beautiful long feather in it. The Renaissance artists painted in the costume of their times. They did not have the money for great research departments such as we have, so that the motion picture is infinitely more correct in its historical detail than Renaissance art or any other art that I know of in painting.

The next point is the camera. The art director now has gone out and is starting his various functions in the 22 departments to bring about the first set. Then comes the camera. The selection of a camera man is vitally important because, in painting, if you were going to do a painting of the battle of Waterloo you would not employ Corot to paint it, because he paints a different type of thing. So with motion pictures, certain camera men are excellent for the pastoral scenes while other camera men are better fitted for dramatic things.

In the matter of lighting I am going to reminisce for a moment to give you an idea of motion picture lighting, because it is a very interesting story and a very important one. I will show you the birth of artificial lighting. When we first went to California, everything was sunlight. No artificial light was employed. Having come from the stage I wanted to get an effect, so I borrowed a spotlight from an old theater in Los Angeles when I was taking a photograph of a spy in *The Warrens of Virginia*. The spy was coming through a curtain and I lighted half of his face only just a smash of light from one side, the other side being dark. I saw the effect on the screen and carried out that idea of lighting all through the rest of the picture, that is, a smash of light from one side or the other, a method that we now use constantly.

When I sent the picture on to the sales department, I received the most amazing telegram from the head of this department saying, "Have you gone mad? Do you expect us to be able to sell a picture for full price when you show only half of the man?" This isn't an exaggeration. This is exactly as it occurred. The exhibitor immediately used that as an argument and said the picture is no good as we showed only half of him. They telegraphed back to me, "We don't know what to do; we can't sell this picture." I was really desperate. As I told you, the director has to go through; he has to do something, so Allah was very kind to me and suggested the phrase "Rembrandt lighting." I sent a telegram to New York saying, "If you fellows are so dumb that you don't know Rembrandt lighting when you see it, don't blame me." The sales department said, "Rembrandt lighting! What a sales argument!" They took the picture out and charged the exhibitor twice as much for it because it had Rembrandt lighting. That is the history of artificial light in motion pictures today.

After the arrangements are made for production, then comes the subject of cast. Is the story strong enough to be portrayed without using a star? Or is it so weak that you must have a great, well known personality that the sales department can sell, in order to overcome the weakness of the story? That is the great struggle for stars too. When a star gets to a point where the sales department can sell him or her, then he or she gets most of the weak stories, because the good stories will sell themselves and the star doesn't need a good story because people will buy a Bill Jones or Susan Smith on the name. The producer, on the other hand, can make a non-star picture with people getting $300 or $400 or $600 a week salary and sell it, saving the weaker material for the star getting $1,000, $2,000, $3,000 or $4,000 a week salary.

We will talk about *The King of Kings* for argument's sake, and say that his subject is big enough so that it requires no star. We send for the casting director and we say, "Here are the types that we want. I am going to require 12 disciples; I am going to require Mary the Mother; I am going to require Mary Magdalen; I am going to require Simon the Cyrenean, and not just people who will necessarily be able to play these parts but people who will sit in the frame of such a picture, not just actors or actresses, but types that are psychologically right." I could talk to you for hours on the theory of casting a picture because it is a very, very important one; it is a very subtle one. It is not "Let us put Mamie in this and let us put Jimmie in that." You have got to make a combination that the public wants to see and that will give you the highest point in artistry because the director is at the point where business and artistry blend. He has to make an artistic piece of work as he sees it for the amount of money which the business department allows him for that picture, so he must fit his cast accordingly. He has to consider the general frame of the picture, and by frame I mean the atmosphere. Then when your cast is selected, tests are made. If it is a big production you have to make camera tests because you cannot trust your judgment in selecting a type for the screen. If possible, you select from the screen first before you see the individual, so that you get the screen personality, because after you meet the individual and then see the screen you instantly translate to the screen the personality that you met, and you do not get the same impression that the audience gets who have not the advantage or disadvantage, as the case may be, of knowing that personality. That is a very, very important point.

The same is true in acting a scene. You cannot judge it with the eye. You do say, but you shouldn't, that it is a great scene; that it was well done; that it will be wonderful. You should see it that night on the screen. So we make tests of characters in makeup and costumes.

When you are bringing together a leading lady from one organization and a leading man who is free lancing, that is, who is engaged in no one company but may be employed by any, the matter of make-up is important. One is accustomed to using one type of make-up and the other is used to another. The cameraman must light for each of these two faces. If he lights for the girl who is very light the man looks like an Arab. If he lights for the man, the woman is pictured entirely white and you cannot see her features at all. There must be a blending, and all that costs a great deal of money, and yet the picture has not started. Up to this point in *The King of Kings* we have spent $200,000, and the camera hasn't turned yet and the financial office is becoming very much worried because they say, "Why, $200,000 has been spent and you have not produced one foot of film. Why?" The wise financial man knows, if he is satisfied with the man at the helm in production, that this is where his foundation is laid.

Then we come to the starting day. All the 22 departments have been functioning and your set is ready. The actors are there in make-up, ready to begin. If you have a great big set, the number of cameras is important because sometimes, if you have, we will say, 200 or 300 people in the set you are working in, you use as many as 14 cameras on one scene, to take your close-ups and long shots at the same time with different lenses. A one-inch lens gives you an enormous field of view. A three-inch lens gives you a close-up. In that way you can match your action for cutting. If in a long shot a man raises his arm to strike somebody, you want to see that blow hit, so you use a three-inch lens centered on that blow. On the long shot, you cut the film from the moment the man raises his hand. Then you put in your close-up shot which just shows the two men, so the audience sees who is struck and who is striking and gets the psychology of it and you come instantly back to your long shot and show the effect of your crowd rushing in to see what has happened. That took a great many years to work out and discover. Your director is leading his orchestra and he works up to a tremendous climax, which is your long shot, holds his orchestra a second, and then your close-up, the short chord of a violin, and back again to your big effect.

The use of a number of cameras is very expensive, so you have to be very sure that you are going to require them. Each camera uses a great deal of film because you photograph this full scene through on your close-up camera, although you are only going to use the pictures actually showing the blow. But when you come to your production that night to study it you find you have two other good moments in there. Therefore, you don't have the man turn just at the moment of the blow, but you have him turn during the entire scene. Your director has to have good judgment for that or he can ruin an organization in the waste of film alone, because it is very expensive and goes very fast and cameramen love to turn the handle.

The next point for the director is the camera line. He looks his set over carefully to see if anything has been neglected, if he can see a blunder of any sort. One thing left out can cause the loss of a whole day's work. We shall say that in the last scene they are going to require a pepper box on the mantelpiece, and that isn't going to be used for four days, and you start in with your first scene. Unless you have in mind that pepper box that you are going to use four days from now and you shoot your first day's work without the pepper box up there, and you come to your last day's work, you have to go back and shoot everything, at an enormous cost.

The director must have the entire vision of the picture completely in mind. He cannot just be thinking of the scene he is going to do. After looking the set over he says O.K. and fixes his camera line. The cameraman doesn't set up and take in the whole set. He approaches it exactly the way an artist does the canvas, as to what is his best position, what will give him the best effect for the dramatic point he is going to bring out. He gets that camera line finally and then calls his people on for rehearsal. If he is a wise director, he rehearses through the camera and he doesn't stand back and tell everybody what to do. He rehearses through the camera because that gives him the picture he is going to see on the screen. If he rehearses without looking through the camera, he gets a big, broad canvas and what he is going to paint is a miniature. Actions viewed outside of the camera and viewed through the camera are frequently entirely different, so that by working through the camera he saves himself frequently a full day because he sees what will appear on the screen and can work from that point.

Then the psychology of the close-up and the long shot is very, very great. A long shot photographs action. A close-up photographs thought. There are some scenes that you must take in close-up and some scenes you must take in long shots. Certain scenes would mean nothing photographed 30 feet away. If I were taking a picture of the gentlemen in the back row, for instance, they could be sound asleep and the camera would never know it. So if I wanted to get the psychology of their reaction to what I am saying I would have to go up and place the camera within seven feet of their faces. Then I would get the expression either of interest or the nod of sound sleep and I would come back here with the camera and go on and the audience would know what the men in the back seat were thinking. That is the way you handle the psychology of that. You jump to the spot where you want to register thought.

The movement of characters can throw you out very easily. In a long shot moving from right to left, when you move your camera in close-up that character must still move from right to left. If it moves from left to right, when you see it on the screen the character meets himself. Those little things cost hundreds and hundreds of dollars if they are overlooked. New angles of camera are important. The Germans are probably the most expert in this respect.

They study and look for new photographic angles to get a different effect. For instance, if I wanted to photograph a hat on the table at my side, if a scene were being made of me and I glanced at that hat I would have to take an insert photograph of the hat in order to let the audience know what I glanced at.

One of the vital things for directors to remember - and here is the greatest temptation- is that you do not teach the actors how to act. The business of a director is not to show everybody how to act, because if he does he inserts his personality into the actor instead of bringing out what the actor has in him; instead of having Ernest Torrence, and Gloria Swanson, and Leatrice Joy, and Rod LaRocque to play the scenes, if I show them what to do I have six or seven little Cecil DeMilles running around. In other words, they are all playing with your personality and are all playing with your ideas instead of your bringing out what is in them.

That is one of the most vital points for a director to know and one of the points that probably few directors really know, because there is a terrible temptation in that quarter. Every director and everybody in this room is confident of being able to act. That is the one weakness of humanity. They all feel they are actors. I don't know why. You do not all feel you are violinists, and yet acting is a great deal harder than playing a violin. There are a great many thousand good violinists. You have them in every orchestra. The great actors you can name on your fingers. Acting pays very much more than playing a violin, so it must be more difficult, and the reason why fewer people reach the top is that they start out with the wrong premise. They start out thinking that acting is easy. It isn't. You are playing a much more delicate instrument than a violin.

The technique of motion picture acting is very great because a camera has no ears. You can say the most magnificent things in the most thrilling way but it cannot hear you. It can only see. Therefore, the voice is useless. You will see a green director insist that his people yell frightfully loud in a mob scene or that the heroine sob terrifically in an emotional scene, and when you see it on the screen you wonder why they all have Saint Vitus dance, because the proper technique is missing.

The principle of screen acting I can give you in one word. If I said, "Do you gentlemen see this yellow paper?" If I said that to the camera, it wouldn't mean anything. I might have said, "There is my watch," or "There is a gentleman taking notes." The screen version of saying that is a moment's pause. That arrests the attention of the audience. Then you pick up the paper, you show it to your audience, you indicate it. Now you know that I am talking about this and you know that I am asking you a question about it. I might yell at the top of my lungs and insist that it is a yellow piece of paper, I and the camera cannot hear it. That, in a word, is the secret of the great screen actors.

Music is an interesting factor in direction. We spend a lot of money to have an orchestra there to put the actor in a certain frame of mind, to get a certain emotional response. That music is just as bad for the director as it is good for the actor, because it fills an emotional spot with him. In watching a scene while an orchestra is playing I always put my hands over my ears, so I will not hear it, because there may be a blank place in the scene which is filled by a beautiful note over here and gives you satisfaction, and when you see it on the screen you say, "Strange I didn't catch that. That point is wrong." The reason is that the music satisfied that void.

The element of time of course is a vital thing. The driving force is the battle with art. A director has to learn to keep two balls in the air at the same time. In the case of *The King of Kings*, the picture cost $19,000 a day to make, for 116 days of shooting time, or $2,225 an hour. You can see what a moment's indecision means. You can see what a little absentmindedness on the part of a director or a property man can mean if he leaves a certain prop at home and if you lose two hours waiting for it you can figure the cost of forgetting Pharaoh's wand. Therefore, your machinery of direction with your assistant directors must be perfect.

Touching that point of the assistant is a very interesting one in the handling of great mobs, where you handle 2,000 and 3,000 people at a time. To get great results you cannot shout at 2,000 or 3,000 people and give them the business to do, and yet each one has to be an actor and do a definite piece of business. The idea of directing a mob scene is not that they all wave their arms, so you divide them up into companies of 100 and you designate one capable assistant director for each hundred. In that hundred extra people he has ten good actors and each actor has ten extra men, and each one of those actors gives the business to the ten extra men and the assistant director gives it to his Centurions or his captains of 100 men, and the assistants get the instructions from the director. That is the way these big mob scenes are handled. They are worked out as mathematically as you would work out an attack on an enemy.

The problems that confront a director are very interesting. To show you the quick thought that a man must have, in the case of the opening of the Red Sea that I spoke of a moment ago, those of you who may have seen the picture remember that you see the children of Israel coming along through the bottom of the sea for about a mile and a half. The exposure took in the walls of water on each side of that and it was in a curve, if you recall. They were driving their flocks of cattle through and if a sheep or cow ran off into the side out of that line, they would run into one of the walls of water. Of course, the walls of water were not there actually. They were on the second exposure of the film, and if the flocks wandered off at all you would be treated to the sight of having a herd of sheep stroll into the ocean. Therefore, we had to build a fence that exactly corresponded to the lines which were to be the walls of water, to keep the cattle inside of those two walls of supposed water. But the fence posts threw a shadow. When we inspected them before shooting, we saw that there were shadows for a mile down in the bottom of the Red Sea, shadows of fence posts. The only thing to do was to shoot it exactly at noon. There were 3,000 people and 8,000 animals in that. That was quite an undertaking. We did it, however, and at 20 minutes before 12 some bright chap came to me and said, "Mister DeMille, do you know the bottom of the Red Sea is dry?" Of course, the sand was dry. Here we had just sent the waters apart and yet the bottom of the sea was perfectly dry. This was 20 minutes before we got ready to turn the camera, and the cost up on that location was $50,000 a day. That meant a full day just to move the animals and people out to that location, which was a long way from camp. So with $50,000 at stake and 20 minutes to do it in I called for a quick suggestion as to how we could darken that sand for two miles. If we get it dark and glistening, we are saved. If that sand is dry and white we are lost. What can we do? Somebody suggested a pump. They had some pumps there. In about 8 of the 20 minutes they wet a strip a few feet in length and as soon as they moved on this place became dry again. I suggested black paint. How much black paint have we got? The painter stepped up and said that there wasn't paint enough in California to paint that.

What would you gentlemen have done? How would you have darkened that sand? We are working by the sea within 40 feet of the shoreline. I will tell you how it was done, because time is pressing. Allah again was very kind. In looking desperately and thinking, "What can I do with this thing?" I saw this great kelp bed at my feet and I said, "Everybody, men, women and children, get up this kelp," and they picked up the kelp and laid kelp for a mile and a half, and at exactly 12:02 we had a nice wet bottom of the sea and we turned the camera. That is the kind of problem that the director is up against and has to solve. If we couldn't have done that, you see what the loss would have been.

I will give you another instance, a rather amusing one. I made a picture once, called *Male and Female*, with Thomas Meighan and Gloria Swanson. Tommy has supposedly just shot a leopard and had it hanging over his shoulder. The property man had a stuffed leopard there with one foot out at one side and the tail going off at an angle. I saw this thing and was terribly annoyed because I had specially talked with the man about it and said, "Get me a body that is limp and will hang as though it were just killed." I had to postpone the shot till the next day, and one of the property men came up and said, "There is a real leopard over in the zoo that just killed a man." I said, "Get me that leopard," because the leopard had to be executed anyway. They have a rule there that one killing is treated as any murder, and the leopard would be killed. I said, "Bring him over here and we will kill him, and Tommy can hold this leopard that has just died, over his shoulder while he plays this impassioned love scene." We brought the leopard over and it was a magnificent animal. I said, "You can't kill that animal. That is a beautiful specimen." Tommy looked a little doubtful. I said, I'll tell you what we'll do. Get a lot of chloroform and ether and some sponges." The property man rushed off and bought all the chloroform and ether in Hollywood and we poured it on these sponges and put it into the leopard's cage, and put something across the front. There was terrible to-do inside the cage, a rocking back and forth and there were frightful noises. Pretty soon everything was quiet and we opened the cage and the leopard was taken out. The scene was all rehearsed and ready. We put the leopard over Tommy's shoulder and said, "All right, Tommy, go ahead." We had men with Winchester 30-30's all around this love scene, and it was rather a long love scene. We had to take it two or three times. Toward the end of the last time - I don't know whether you gentlemen know all about ether - you probably know more about it than I do; I don't know whether you ever heard anyone coming out of ether or chloroform or a mixture of the two, but this mixture has a strange effect, and in the middle of the love scene this leopard started. He was perfectly unconscious, but you have heard people talk under the influence of ether. Well, this leopard talked and talked in the middle of this impassioned love scene, and Tommy, with Gloria's hand pressed on his heart said, "Mr. DeMille, I tell you he is coming to."

I will give you another instance of what a director must inspire in his people, a different story, to show you the esprit de corps of the motion picture profession, and I know of nothing that will better show it to you. When that camera turns it is the wheel of fate.

I was shooting a scene in *The Little American* and we were firing a line of guns, supposedly French 75's. As they were using the real ones over in France we had to use imitations. In the middle of this scene the breech-block blew out of one of these guns and one man had a portion of his anatomy torn away, another had a great splinter go through his mouth and tear out his cheek; that whole gun crew was shot to pieces. But there wasn't one of those men that stopped acting. There wasn't a man on either side that turned to those fellows. They glanced at them as you would if it had been a real shell that struck and went on with their own guns until that scene was played through and the whistle blew. Then they went to these men.

Men will give their lives, gentlemen, to carry through. Nothing will stop them. They will do anything.

Cecil B. DeMille, "Motion Picture Directing," *Transactions of S.M.P.E.*, Volume 12, No. 34, 1928, pages 295-309.

APPENDIX D

The Screen as a Religious Teacher

How the Much-Discussed Filming of The King of Kings, the New Religious Drama, Was Produced with Reverence and Accuracy

By Cecil B. DeMille

To give the peoples of the modern world the same opportunity to see the wondrous life-drama of Jesus as was given to the citizens of Judea nineteen hundred years ago has been the object of my endeavors in making *The King of Kings*. My purpose is, of course, dramatic entertainment; drama in its highest sense as defined in the immortal apothegm of Aristotle. And in this connection I wish to refer to the assemblage of representatives of more than thirty religious sects and beliefs who gathered at the studio last August, opening the film-taking with a service of prayer.

What brought these ministers of conflicting faiths together? Not only all the religions believed in by European peoples and Americans were represented, but also the Buddhist and Mohammedan faiths. It was the first time in history that two of the sects had ever appeared together in public. The reason for their friendly, co-operating presence lay in the belief of these religious leaders that the motion-picture medium possessed the power to carry the story of Jesus to millions who might not otherwise be sympathetic to it, or who would find difficulty in grasping it because of racial or linguistic reasons.

A dozen years ago such an attempt as mine would have been impossible. Movies then would have been regarded as too cheap and banal a medium, whereas today they are associated with the greatest of themes and embody the thoughts of many of the world's greatest thinkers. Twelve years ago the subject would not have appealed for another reason, namely, that religion was a thing conventionally accepted by the great majority of people, but too often disregarded. The World War shook everything to its foundations. Old standards and old ideas would not fit, and new theories and principles were strained after, only to be found worthless. The same people are groping today for a foundation, for proven standards of acceptance. The ideals of the Man of Nazareth have persisted throughout all the centuries, and there is an almost universal demand for the return to greater knowledge of Him and the influence of His mission. The power of the screen as a vital factor in education has been thoroughly proven. Consequently the focusing of this power on the teachings of Jesus will be of tremendous value.

I am not referring only to those who are termed Christians. The fundamental truths brought out through the ministry of Jesus cannot be confined to belief, race, nationality or social position. Whether he believes that Jesus was a divine being who descended to humanity or a human being who rose to divinity, it is not after all tremendously important in view of the fact that His ideals apply to all of us.

Thus, it is our earliest desire to offend no one's religious beliefs, but to benefit uncounted millions of the world's population by telling of the Ministry, Crucifixion and Resurrection of Jesus - the greatest story ever told. It was with the utmost humility that I approached this subject, and it was with the deepest reverence that the work of visualizing it was done.

Permit me to illustrate this fact by two or three happenings among the sets or on location which demonstrate the power of the scenes over those who worked in their midst. When we were filming Jesus teaching the Lord's Prayer to the assembled multitude on the temple steps, there followed a moment's silence, after which the set orchestra played softly the Doxology. Moved by the emotion of the scene, one of the players began to sing the words, and immediately the entire group, numbering a thousand, spontaneously chorused the soul-stirring song in unison.

On another occasion, as we were closing our work of representing the beautiful scenes of the Resurrection and the hour approached Christmas Eve, the great pipe organ on the set pealed forth one after another of the loved carols of Yuletide. The actors and actresses forgot themselves and sang these carols as their religious forebears had sung them in front of the churches and homes of Merrie England centuries ago.

The children who were on the set for the six or eight months of our picture-taking received a religious education the equivalent of at least two or three years' plodding attendance in a Bible class. I believe it will be found that, just as appropriate motion pictures greatly shorten the pupils' acquirement of the essential factors of history, geography and other literary studies, so Bible pictures will enable the boys and girls to get the outlines of the Old and New Testament stories in briefest time with the greatest pleasure and delight and with the utmost reverence for the subjects and the arousing of the religious emotions.

At no time in the world's history has humanity so hungered for the truth. Science has declared there is a God. And a groping, eager world, cries, "How may we find Him?"

The answer goes back two thousand years, to a Man who stood with a little band of ragged followers in the midst of bigotry, cruelty and ignorance lighting with the torch of His own life the flame of hope in the heart of man and showing us by sublime Sacrifice- Death and Resurrection- our own Immortality.

Cecil B. De Mille, "The Screen as a Religious Teacher," *Theatre*, June 1927, pages 45, 76.

APPENDIX E

C.B. DeMille, An Epic Biopic of Cecil B. DeMille and the Creation of Hollywood

By Robert Hammond

LOGLINE: Cecil B. DeMille struggles to bring his epic vision to the big screen against the restraints of his financial backer and the temptations of Hollywood.

TAGLINE: The man who invented Hollywood.

PREMISE: Creativity overcomes commercialism.

GENRE: Epic biopic in the vein of *The Aviator, A Beautiful Mind,* and *Walk the Line.*

C.B. DEMILLE is an epic biopic of the pioneering director, Cecil B. DeMille and the establishment of Hollywood as the film capital of the world.

DeMille was a born showman, one of the most prolific and successful directors of all time, and the man who was most responsible for turning Hollywood into the world's film capitol. As the creative force behind Paramount Studios, DeMille handled every existing film genre and formulated some that never existed before, most notably the Biblical epic. DeMille is the story of his struggle to make Biblical epics against the greed of New York moneymen and the allure of California starlets.

While creating a unique portrayal of DeMille, the story also pays homage to his appearance in the Billy Wilder film, *Sunset Boulevard* (Paramount, 1950. Because the majority of DeMille's films and his work centered on Paramount Studios (which DeMille began in a barn along with co-founders Jesse Lasky and Adolph Zukor), the story incorporates the making of such films as *The Ten*

Commandments (1923 and 1956 versions) as well as *Sampson and Delilah*.

The central struggle in the film is between director DeMille and producer Adolph Zukor. Whereas DeMille is primarily concerned with making movies, Zukor's main goal is making money. The juxtaposition between diametrical forces of creativity and fear establishes an ongoing conflict. Subplots include relationships with DeMille's other partners Jesse Lasky and Sam Goldwyn as well as DeMille's relationship with his daughter Ciddy (Cecilia), his wife Constance and his two mistresses, scenario writer Jeanie Macpherson and actress Julia Faye. While creating and promoting films espousing Judeo-Christian morality, DeMille struggles with his own sins of adultery, anger, and dishonesty. Hence, we have a story of an ordinary man who overcomes relentless obstacles to become a legend.

READER NOTES:

"The theme of DeMille concerns how we, as human beings, deal with our love of life, family and friends."

"This is the best script that I have read in the past

year. There is a whimsy and lightheartedness about the whole piece which makes it a pleasure to read and hard to put down."

"The pace of this script is fast. The action and dialogue flow very well in each scene and set up a compelling visual story."

"The idea of bringing the story of DeMille's life to the screen is extremely intriguing and appealing. It has the potential of exploring a seemingly complicated man and his artistic vision."

ABOUT THE AUTHOR

Robert Hammond

Robert Hammond has authored numerous self-help books and is a popular national speaker on the subject of personal and professional achievement. He has appeared on over 300 radio and television programs. He has an MFA in Creative Writing, teaches screenwriting, and develops literary properties for film and television.

Hammond's bestselling book, *Life After Debt: Free Yourself from the Burdens of Money Worries – Once and for All* sold over 100,000 copies.

As the author of *Identity Theft: How to Protect Your Most Valuable Asset,* Hammond was the spokesperson for Capital One Financial Corporation's Identity Theft Prevention Program.

Hammond is also a screenwriter, producer, and creative executive, with multiple film credits including the award-winning screenplay, *C.B. DeMille* based on his novel.